RESPONSA
and
HALAKHIC STUDIES

RESPONSA
and
HALAKHIC STUDIES

by

ISAAC KLEIN

KTAV PUBLISHING HOUSE, INC.
1975

Library of Congress Cataloging in Publication Data

Klein, Isaac.
   Responsa and halakhic studies.

   Includes bibliographical references.
   1. Responsa—1800. 2. Halakhah—Collected works.
3. Jewish law—Collected works. I. Title
BM522.59.L37   296.1'79   75-25634
ISBN 0-87068-288-1

MANUFACTURED IN THE UNITED STATES OF AMERICA

TABLE OF CONTENTS

PREFACE

This book is divided into three sections: The first section consists of responsa that were written for the law committee of the Rabbinical Assembly of which I have been a member since 1935; the second part, of short answers to halakhic questions addressed to me by colleagues and culled from my correspondence with them, of which I have chosen at random from the large number in my files; the third section contains studies I prepared for delivery at Rabbinical Assembly conventions and conferences, with the exception of the one entitled "Science and Some Ethical Issues," which was prepared for the Institute of Ethics of the Institute for Religion and Social Studies of the Jewish Theological Seminary.

A number of these papers are dated and would need some revision in order to be brought up to date. In a few cases, my opinion has changed, and some suffer from the fact that much new material on the subject has since become available. After due deliberation, I thought it best to leave the material as it was when presented.

Thanks are due to many who have helped me in the publication of this book: Temple Shaarey Zedek of Buffalo, where I served as rabbi from 1953 to 1974 and now as Rabbi Emeritus, and its members whose many kindnesses and whose consideration have made it possible for me to continue to study while in the active and busy rabbinate; Hollywood Temple Beth El of Los Angeles, where I worshipped during the last two winters, its members and, especially, its most kind rabbi, Rabbi Joseph Wagner, who, during this time, have made me feel most welcome and allowed me to use their facilities for my work; and to Henriette, my life's companion, for being a constant source of inspiration and encouragement.

1. CIVIL MARRIAGE (1938)

QUESTION: *What is the status of civil marriage according to Jewish law?*

ANSWER: The question that we propose to discuss in this paper deals with the problem of civil marriage. What is the status of civil marriage according to Jewish law? Is a civil marriage valid that was performed at court or before a justice of the peace so that a *get* would be necessary for the couple to separate according to Jewish law, or does civil marriage have no standing at all, so that we consider the parties unmarried? Should these parties thus married in a civil ceremony and then divorced in court come before a rabbi in order to remarry? What course should they pursue? Should they consider themselves unmarried according to the Jewish law and eligible to be married, or must the rabbi refuse to officiate on the grounds that as far as the Jewish law is concerned, she is still a married woman, an *eshet ish,* and he is a married man?

This is a long-standing question that has been appearing with increasing frequency since the time that the state declared marriage to lie within its domain. With the rapid secularization of life and the weakening of the hold of religious practices upon the people, more and more couples resort to the privilege of marrying by a civil marriage without the benefit of a religious wedding as prescribed by Jewish law.

In the past, when marriage was considered entirely a matter for the religious authorities and, among the Jews, a matter to be taken care of by the Jewish community, such a question could not have arisen. Yet, we do find certain analogous cases even in the past. During the Spanish Inquisition, Marrano Jews would often be married according to the law of the Church. They could not get married according to Jewish law for obvious reasons. The difference between such cases and the civil marriage of today lies in the fact that whereas with Marranos it was a matter of compulsion, with us it is a voluntary act. Somewhat similar to the case of the Marranos is the case of civil marriage in Soviet Russia. There, although

1

freedom of religion is officially the law of the land and there is no pressure to forego a religious marriage, yet there are strong social and often indirect economic pressures which force people to abstain from religious observance. Many couples omit the religious marriage ceremony for fear of losing caste. The problem comes before the religious authorities when partners to such a marriage emigrate, and inquire whether their marriage is valid enough to require a *get* if they wish to marry again. Most pressing and most common is the problem in Western Europe and America where these cases are voluntary in nature, and come before us with increasing frequency.

At *prima facie,* it would seem that the civil marriage must be ruled entirely invalid. In the Mishnah we read: "There are three instruments of marriage: money, a document, and the marital act." (Mishnah Kiddushin 1:1) Under which of these three categories can we class civil marriage? It cannot be classed under the first, because during the marriage proceedings the groom does not give the bride anything of the value of a *perutah.* It cannot fit into the second category because, although there is a legal document involved in the process, it is of no value to us since, according to the prescription of the Jewish law, it must contain a definite formula and must be given by the groom to the bride, which is not the case in civil marriage. It cannot come under the third category, because the marital act does not come under consideration here.

It may be suggested that the consummation of the marriage which follows should serve as the instrument of marriage as suggested in the third category, but we must discount this suggestion, because of a very explicit statement in the Tosefta which reads: "Every marital act that is [consummated] with the intention that it constitute marriage, we count it a valid marriage, and every marital act which is not with the intention that it be an instrument of marriage, the marriage is not valid." (*Tosefta* Kiddushin 1:3) The codes are also very explicit in regards to our case. We will cite only the passage in the *Shulhan Arukh* of R. Joseph Karo that refers to it. It reads: "And likewise, a man and a woman, who because of violent hostility to the Jews have become apostates and married according to the laws of the Gentiles, even though they are seen in private every day without any effort to hide it from people there is not the slightest reason to consider their marriage valid" (*Eben ha-Ezer* 149:6).

A further examination of the sources, however, may lead us to modify our conclusion. In spite of the clear indication that civil marriage is not valid, there are certain points of law to consider which will prompt us to change our view. Of great importance to us in this case is the principle *ein adam oseh b'ilato b'ilat zenut,* which means, in effect, that we take it for granted wherever possible that people will prefer to make their intercourse licit rather than illicit. In the case of a woman who is not married to the man, it would imply that intercourse would become an instrument of marriage rather than of an illicit relationship. We will cite three cases in the Talmud where the principle is applied that have some affinity to the problem under consideration.

A. In the case of a divorced couple that spent the night at a lodging house in privacy, so that we have reason to believe that they lived again as husband and wife, it is the opinion of the school of Shammai that the status quo is not changed, but it is the opinion of the school of Hillel that we consider them remarried and that in order to separate again a *get* would be necessary. Rabba bar bar Hanah in the name of Rabbi Yohanan said that the difference of opinion between the school of Shammai and the school of Hillel is based upon the opposing views they hold regarding the principle of *ein adam oseh b'ilato b'ilat zenut.* According to the school of Shammai, in this case, it is quite conceivable that relations should be illicit, while the school of Hillel holds that we should apply the principle, and declare the act to have been committed with the intention of marriage (B. Gittin 81a).

B. A groom made certain conditions to his bride at the betrothal, upon whose fulfillment the validity of the marriage would depend. At the consummation of the marriage, however, the groom, disregarded the conditions he had made and did not demand that they be fulfilled. It is the opinion of Rab that in such a case a *get* is necessary, whereas Shmuel believes that no *get* is required under these circumstances. Abayei interprets the opinion of Rab and claims that Rab does not mean to say that when the groom failed to mention the conditions at the consummation of the marriage he thereby repudiated them and thereby no longer made the

validity of the marriage dependent upon them. The reason for the
opinion of Rab is that whenever possible, a person would not want
to make his relations illicit, but would rather consider it a marital
act. (B. Ketubbot 72b)

C. In cases where the performance of the marriage is marred
by certain errors of omission according to the law—as, for instance,
if the object that the groom gives to the bride does not have the
value of the *perutah*, the minimum value required by the law, or if
the groom was a minor—even if the groom should send gifts to the
bride afterward which might be construed as intending to serve as
an instrument of marriage, yet the marriage is not valid. If, however, there were marital relations afterward, they are considered
married in spite of the fact that the original marriage performance
did not meet with the requirements of the law. (B. Ketubbot 73b)

These instances would indicate that although common-law marriages are not valid according to Jewish law, yet if they are preceded by certain acts which would suggest that the marriages are
intended to be legitimate, we rely upon the principle of *ein adam
oseh b'ilato b'ilat zenut* and assume that their relations were entered into with the definite intention of marriage and, therefore,
though strongly discouraged by rabbinic law, the marital act constitutes a legal and valid marriage. The case of civil marriage is
very similar. The process in court, though of no value by itself
from the point of view of Jewish law, yet would at least indicate
that the people wanted to be married and live as husband and wife,
in which case we have a right to assume the principle of *ein adam
oseh b'ilato b'ilat zenut* and consider the marriage valid enough to
necessitate a *get*.

Several objections may be raised to the conclusion we have thus
arrived at:

1. First, we have the question of witnesses. The function of witnesses at the marriage ceremony is not identical with the function
of witnesses in the case of other transactions. Testimony in litiga-
tions, in money transactions, in the certification of documents is a
matter of prudence. Where the parties concerned have perfect trust
in each other, where no conflict arises, the very same transactions
are valid without witnesses. The Talmud expresses this idea in this
principle: *Hoda'at ba'al din k'me'ah eidim damie.* "The admission
of the litigant is as good as the testimony of a hundred witnesses."

Even better is the function of witnesses in cases of litigation illustrated by this incident told in the Talmud: "Mar Zutro and Rab Adda Saba, sons of Rab Mari bar Isur, divided their possessions among themselves. They came before Rab Ashi and said to him: 'Does the biblical law of two witnesses mean that they are needed so that in case one of the parties desires to change his mind he may not do so, and in our case this will not happen? Or does it mean that the transaction is not valid unless there are two witnesses?' He answered them, 'Witnesses were created for liars'" (B. Kiddushin 65b). Witnesses are a precautionary measure, here, to prevent any of the parties from backing out or from denying the truth. Under these circumstances, the witnesses are, *eidei beirur,* a means of clarifying and verifying the situation. In marriage, the function of the witnesses is not only to bear testimony to the fact that these people were legally married; the witnesses are an integral part of the process—they are part and parcel of the marriage instrument. The absence of witnesses does not merely mean that should a conflict arise we shall be at a disadvantage, but also that the marriage ceremony was incomplete and not performed in accordance with the prescription of the law. In the Talmud this expresses itself in this passage: "Said Rab Nachman in the name of Shmuel, The marriage of him who marries in the presence of one witness is not valid even if both parties admit that they were married" (B. Kiddushin 65a). In the case of marriage the witnesses are *eidi kiyum* or *eidei pe'ulah.* Their testimony is part of the act that validates it. In all the cases cited from the Talmud, there are witnesses present during the privacy preceding marital relations. According to the accepted principle of *hen hen eidei yihud, hen hen eidei bi'ah* this is sufficient. In our case, there are no witnesses present at all. It may be suggested that we assume that at some time there must have been some *eidei yihud* present. They may have had some visitors who stayed late in the evening and left when it was time to retire. These would be analogous to the *eidei yihud* that we have in the cases cited from the Talmud. We have no right, however, to make such assumptions, because in the case of marriage, the law requires that the witnesses be appointed with the express intention of witnessing a legal act. (RITBO, Kiddushin 46, Makkot 10).

2. The second objection is based upon an opinion of Maimonides who says: "Some gaonic authorities have rendered the decision

that any woman who has had relations with a man in the presence of witnesses needs a *get*, because we take it for granted that rather than have illicit relations the parties prefer that the act constitute marriage." "These Geonim," continues Maimonides, "do not merit our consideration of their stand, because this principle of the Talmud applies only to the cases mentioned in the Talmud, i.e., a divorced woman who had marital relations with her divorced husband, and in a case where the act was preceded by betrothal, but with conditions attached. In these cases, where there were already some connections, we take the stand that the relations were licit, unless the parties expressly say they were illicit. In other circumstances, we take the opposite stand, that unless the parties defiitely express that their intention is marriage, we consider the relations illicit" (*Mishneh Torah*, Laws Concerning Divorce 6:19).

In all the cases cited from the Talmud there was some act preceding intercourse which justified our assumption that the relations were licit. In the case of the divorced couple, their coming together in a lodging house is an indication that they have decided to come together again. In the second instance, there are actual *kiddushin*, though with strings attached, preceding the act. In our case, since we discount the ceremony in court because it is of no value from the point of view of Jewish law, it would seem that we cannot invoke the principle of *ein adam oseh b'ilato b'ilat zenut*.

3. The third objection is that of Rabbi Isaac ben Sheshet commonly known as the Rivosh. In his collection of responsa there is a case of Marranos who were married in church by a priest. It is a question analogous to our own. His decision is that no *get* is necessary, because: "Even according to those gaonic authorities who believe that under ordinary circumstances we assume that the relations were with the intention that it constitute marriage according to Jewish law, in our case, where the beginning was made according to the laws of the Gentiles, it is as if they had explicitly declared that their intentions were not to be married according to the Law of Moses and of Israel, but according to the laws of the Gentiles." (*She'eilot u'Teshuvot ha-Rivash*, responsum 6) It is a case of *mahshavto nikeret m'tokh ma'asov*: His act reveals his intention. Now, if, in the case of Marranos where one has no choice in the matter, we still take it as an indication of an objection to religious marriage, in the case of civil marriage, where this course

is chosen voluntarily, we certainly have to assume it as an indication of an objection to being married *kedat Mosheh v'Yisroel*.

4. The fourth objection is based upon the question of intention. In the Talmud, there is the following case which is apropos: "An orphaned female minor, who did not go through the process of *mi'un* has matured and has married another man. Rab says that she does not need a *get* from the second man (because the marriage with the first was a valid marriage) ; and Shmuel, that she needs a *get* from the second man (because the marriage with the first man was not a valid marriage). What were the circumstances here? Were there marital relations? If there were marital relations, why, then, does Shmuel maintain that the marriage with the first man was not valid? Because Shmuel is of the opinion that the relations relied for their legitimacy upon the first marriage when she was a minor, and when the marriage was not binding" (B. Yebamot 109b).

In this case the opinion of Rab and Shmuel is based upon the question of whether the man's intentions were for the act to constitute an instrument of marriage. Rab is of the opinion that the man was aware of the fact that the marriage, when she was a minor, was not valid and thus his decision that the consummation that comes when the wife reaches maturity should constitute marriage. Shmuel, on the contrary, maintains that the parties believed that their original marriage was legal to all intents and purposes, and his marital relations, therefore, are not with the intent that they constitute marriage, but rather that of already full-fledged husband and wife. Their marriage, therefore, is not valid. It seems, then, that very much, if not all, depends upon the intention and the state of mind of the parties concerned. What do the parties to a civil marriage take their marital relations to be? When a couple takes out a marriage license they know that they are still unmarried. When, however, they are married in court, being aware that the law that is binding and that remarrying after this would constitute bigamy, they feel that they are fully husband and wife. It is thus evident, that any relationship that follows is in the nature of the relation of husband and wife. Our judgment upon the validity of their marriage cannot, therefore, depend upon the marital act that follows, but upon the process of the court.

5. The fifth objection is based upon another opinion of Mai-

monides. According to Maimonides, the principle of *ein adam oseh b'ilato b'ilat zenut* applies only to people who abide by the law and Jewish moral standards. People whose moral principles are dubious naturally cannot come within this category. People who do not submit to a religious marriage are counted among those to whom the principle would not apply. (*Mishneh Torah* Laws Concerning Divorce, 7:23; Laws Concerning Estates, 7:23; *Terumat haDeshen*, responsum 209)

We will now try to answer these questions in the order that they were presented, *al rishon rishon, v'al ahron ahron*. The first objection raised was the absence of witnesses. It is not at all sure, however, that in the case of marriage the witnesses are not *eidei beirur*. We have ample reason to believe that the matter is not at all settled. There are a number of passages in the Talmud that would suggest that in marriage, too, the witnesses are *eidei beirur*. We shall cite cases where that is very evident.

a. "The court punishes in cases where there is *hazakah* even though there are no witnesses (B. Kiddushin 80a). To illustrate this, the Talmud gives this example: "A man and a woman, a boy and a girl, that grew up in the same house, that is proof enough that they are husband and wife, father and mother, or brother and sister, and the relationship between them, i.e., the man and the girl, or the woman and the boy, or the boy and the girl, are incestuous, and the court can on this basis mete out the prescribed punishment" (ibid). It seems that all we are concerned about here is the testimony that the relations are that of husband and wife. Since we have this testimony from their manner of living, no witnesses are necessary.

b. We have further evidence from the law of *kol*, a rumor. We read: "If a rumor in town circulates that she is married, we follow the rumor and consider her married (B. Gittin 88b). In the code of R. Joseph Karo, we read: "If a rumor circulates in town about an unmarried woman that she was married today to this and this individual, we heed that rumor, and consider it a marriage about the validity of which there is some doubt, even though there is no clear proof about it" (*Eben ha-Ezer* 46:1). In this case, too, it is evident that it is a question of ordinary testimony. If it were a matter of *eidei pe'ulah* a rumor would not be sufficient to necessitate a *get*.

c. We also have reason to believe that when a matter is something known to all there is no need for *eidei yihud*. In the Bet
Shmuel, a commentary on the *Eben ha-Ezer* of Karo, we read: If
he married her and it is known to all, it is counted as if witnesses
were present at the marital act. Accordingly, if it is known to all
that he took her with the intentions of marriage, we count the
intercourse as the instrument of marriage. (Bet Shmuel 26:1).
The Gaon of Vilna comments on the same place: "Although there
were not any *eidei yihud* since everyone knows of their privacy, we
take it as a certainty that there were intentions of marriage behind
the act."

As to the objection that we have no right to assume that at some
time there must have been *eidei yihud* present because these must
be appointed especially for that function, the answer is that the
necessity for appointment has no basis in law but is rather a
minhag based on precaution. The law explicitly states: "If the
marriage was performed before witnesses even if he did not tell
them, 'You are my witnesses,' the marriage is valid." (*Eben ha-Ezer*
42:4). and further we read: "And even if he appointed witnesses,
others who were present are eligible to testify" (ibid., in Ramo).

d. Maimonides' objection that the principle of *ein adam oseh
b'ilato b'ilat zenut* applies only to those cases mentioned in the
Talmud, does not apply to civil marriage. His objection is valid only
in the case of *panui ha-ba al hapnu'yah* when the affair is between
an unmarried man and an unmarried woman who did not declare
their intention to get married. In such a case we cannot apply the
principle because in those instances in the Talmud where the principle is applied, there always is some previous arrangement that
would lead us to believe that the parties concerned desire to become
husband and wife. In those instances where this previous arrangement very obviously foreshadows marriage, even the school of
Shammai, which opposes the principle of *ein adam oseh b'ilato b'ilat
zenut*, admits that we apply it. (B. Kiddushin 81a, in Tosafot, s.v.,
Beit Shamai).

In the case of civil marriage, the ceremony in court has at least
the value of such an introductory act. It certainly cannot be counted
less than *meshudekhet*, a declared match or an engagement, as we
term it. In the case of a couple that has been engaged, we do not
put them in that category of *panui ha-ba al hapnu'yah*, where we

do not apply the principle, but among those instances which the Talmud mentions where, because of an act preceding marital relations, we apply the principle of *ein adam oseh b'ilato b'ilat zenut*. (*Sheilot u-Teshuvot RDBZ*, responsum 1287; *Arukh ha-Shulhan, Eben ha-Ezer* 148:8). We have all the reason to apply the principle in our case where the law of the land make the process in the court much more binding than an engagement, and the man and the woman are certainly going to be husband and wife. The objection of Maimonides can further be rejected by the comment the RABD makes. The RABD claims that Maimonides' objection applies only to those who are *beheskat pritsut*, people who are known to be wanton violators of moral standards, but does not apply to decent people.

Furthermore, although Maimonides' opinion is the accepted one, we cannot disregard entirely the opposing opinion of the gaonic authorities, especially since such a later authority as Mordecai upholds the opinion of the Geonim. (*Mordekhai* Kiddushin, Perek ha-Omer, piska 533). In that case we apply the principle even when there is no preceding act to suggest that these wish to become husband and wife, and, certainly, in the case of civil marriage.

c. The objection based on the opinion of Rabbi Isaac ben Sheishet that *mahshabto nikeret mitokh ma-a sov* is the best indication that they do not desire to be married *kedat Mosheh v'Yisroel*, according to the Law of Moses and of Israel, does not apply to our case. Let us see what the mental attitude is of the parties that go through a civil marriage. Is it a matter of *l'hakhit* ("spite"), or just a passive disregard of the requirements of the Jewish law? In most cases it is safe to assume that the parties do not object to a religious marriage. If we should tell them that with their civil marriage they also satisfy the religious requirements, they will not file a protest. In many cases it is a sheer case of ignorance. Often young people simply do not know what the procedure is. Many of them are so far removed from Jewish life that they do not even know that a civil marriage is not enough in Jewish law. Under these circumstances, we surely cannot assume that the parties have definite objections to being married *k'Dat Mosheh v'Yisroel*.

d. The fourth objection, although based on good logic, is not accepted by Jewish law. This reasoning, which we drew from a passage in the Talmud, is based on an opinion of Shmuel. Rab,

however, opposes this view, and the final decision of the law favors
the opinion of Rab. The reason behind it is that in applying the
principle of *ein adam oseh b'ilato b'ilat zenut* we emphasize the
fact that a person will, wherever possible, do the right thing and
will rather act in a way that will be licit and legitimate. In this
case, to be licit the relations must be considered as the marital act,
the instrument of marriage. Rab is, therefore, of the opinion that
we consider the relations were performed with the intention of
marriage.

e. The last objection cannot be entertained today, for reasons
that we have already referred to. Obviously, when we come to judge
who are *kesheirim* we cannot abide by one standard all the time.
Nonobservance of the laws of *niddah* and *mikvah* are mentioned as
putting one outside of *kesheirim*. It is obvious that we cannot adhere to this criterion today, not only for those who dispense with
religious marriage, but also among those who are very scrupulous
that the marriage be performed strictly according to the requirements of Jewish law. Our experience is that the moral standards of
those who have become united through civil marriage, as far as
marital fidelity and the purity of their family life, is concerned,
compares very favorably with the standards of those who have had
the benefit of a religious marriage.

According to the law then, our decision is that in the case of civil
marriage a *get* is necessary. Since, however, there are numerous
authorities who are of the opinion that a *get* is not necessary, we
must also consider the practical implications of our conclusion.
What effect will our attitude have upon the sanctity of marriage
and the integrity of the family? It is pointed out that by necessitat-
ing a *get* in the case of civil marriage, we put our stamp of approval
upon it, and thus encourage it. This reasoning is a bit far-fetched.
The Rabbis in the Talmud never hesitated to require a *get* where
there was the slightest touch of *kidushei safek* (marriage of doubt-
ful validity). On the other hand, we must take into consideration
the fact that if a *get* were not to be required, we would cast a
shadow of illegitimacy upon a large number of families—a very
serious practical objection. We know that most of the people that
rest content with a civil marriage will not apply for a *get* when
they wish to separate; they will remain content with a legal divorce.
It is very common even among couples that insisted upon a religious

marriage, that they dispense with the *get* and get only a legal civil divorce—and certainly couples married in court, will not bother to obtain a *get*. Should we consider the civil marriage valid enough to require a *get*, then a woman who was thus married is an *eshet ish* even after she has received a legal civil divorce. Should she marry again, she would be commiting adultery.

Furthermore, if we consider the woman who has been married in court an *eshet ish*, a full-fledged married woman, we add to the already grave *agunah* problem. Should the husband desert the wife after he has received a legal divorce, the status of the woman in the community will be that of one more *agunah*.

These objections are very strong, and must be considered. It is our impression, however, that we would cause more harm if we should decide that a *get* is not necessary. As for the problem of the *agunah*, if that should come up, we would adhere to the rabbinic tradition of stretching the law as far as possible to relieve the plight of the woman. Here, too, we would have to resort to a *heter* which is supplied to us by many great authorities. In all other cases, we should decide that a *get* is necessary.

In conclusion, let me quote from a letter of Rabbi B. Shapiro, Chief Rabbi of Kovno: "All facets of the doubt are known and the decisions of the rabbis are manifest. I believe, however, that a general subject like this that has an exalted place in the world of faith and is the main foundation of family life, and draws with it the question of the illegitimacy of children, must not be judged by individuals, each one according to his individual opinion. For if such is the procedure, the Torah becomes as two Torahs, and the house of Israel is torn into segments, for one rabbi will permit and will act accordingly, with the result that children will be born, and when they come to a place where the rabbis are inclined to be stricter, they will consider them as illegitimate, and there is no remedy, God forbid. Therefore there is, according to my opinion, an urgent need, that this question, and others like it, should be solved possibly, either through the conference of a major number of Torah scholars, or at least, and in an emergency, by correspondence" (*Hapardes*, v.8. no. 11).

2. THE PROBLEM OF HALIṢAH (1969)

The disruption of the traditional pattern of Jewish life has not spared the sanctity that was once characteristic of Jewish family life, a great number of breaches have appeared in the ramparts that guarded it. As a result, many new problems arose in the laws regulating marriage and the family and many of the old problems came to the fore again with a sharper edge and with greater urgency. Among these is the problem of *haliṣah*.

The childless widow who is liable to *haliṣah* has often been subjected to indignities and injustices (See Kahana, I.S., *Sefer ha-Agunot*, 5714, p. 57 for examples). In our day, in the diaspora, where the rabbi and the *beth din* have no coercive power and must therefore rely completely on persuasion to implement their decisions, instances of extortion and blackmail are almost inevitable. Other difficulties that contribute to the misery of the woman liable for *halitza* arise when the levir who is under obligation to submit to *halitza* is not legally of the age required for its execution, thus making the widow into an *agunah* until he becomes of age, and when the whereabout of the levir is unknown, or if he lives in a faraway country. (There is a recent case of a minor levir who was exempted from *haliṣah* by the chief rabbis of Israel—but this was a special case because the original marriage was not consummated due to the husband's impotence. (*Hadashot*, Department of Religious Information, Hekhal Shlomo, no. 58–59, February–March 1967 p.1.)

The new aspect of the problem is that today, even when no difficulty is involved fewer and fewer men and women are willing to submit to this obligation. The procedure has become repugnant and meaningless to the modern temper. Both the rabbis who arrange for the *haliṣah* and the parties who execute it find the experience unpleasant and revolting. The question then is whether a way could be found within the framework of the traditional halakha, to make *haliṣah* nonobligatory.

We cannot accept the Reform position based on a resolution passed by the Synod held at Augsburg, in 1871, and by the Conference of American Rabbis in Philadelphia, in 1869 to the effect that, "The biblical precept concerning *haliṣah* has lost its importance, since the circumstances which occasioned the levirate marriage and *haliṣah* no longer exist, and the idea underlying the whole precept has become foreign to our religious and social views.

The nonperformance of *haliṣah* is no impediment to the widow's remarriage" (Mielziner, Moses, The Jewish Law of Marriage and Divorce, Bloch, N. Y. 1901, p. 58).

This obviously is not the traditional halakhic approach. Nor can we accept the suggestion that *haliṣah* should be eliminated since levirate marriage, for which *haliṣah* is only a substitute, has already been eliminated, (See Rabbinical Assembly Proceedings, 1952, p. 153ff.). This suggestion has no merit according to Halakhah since the discontinuance of levirate marriage was not only not adopted by all Jewish communities, but even where it was adopted it was only on a *de facto* and not a *de jure* basis. Theoretically it is still in force, but *haliṣah* has been given priority over it. We shall have more about this further.

Ever since the adoption of the *Herem d'Rabbenu Gershom,* levirate marriage is feasible when the levir is single and in countries where the *herem* is not accepted. (See such cases cited below). All authorities agree that the law of levirate marriage is still in force; they disagree only on the question of which has priority, levirate marriage or *haliṣah*. (B. Yebamot 39b, *Eben ha-Ezer* 161:1, *Be'er ha-Golah*, ad loc. *Dinei Nisuim v'Gerushin,* P. Dykan-Dickstein, p. 152)

This question of priority is based on the following mishnaic statement:

> Formerly, the duty of levirate marriage came before the duty of *haliṣah* when the intent of the act was to fulfill a religious duty: but now when the intent of the act is not to fulfill a religious duty, it has been enjoined that the duty of *halisah* comes before the duty of levirate marriage (Bekhorot 1:7).

Professor Hanokh Albeck comments on this: "As far as practice is concerned; however, no rigid rules have been set in this law. There are some who gave priority to levirate marriage over *halisah*. There were also various customs in the time of the geonim. In Sura the custom was to have levirate marriage, while in Pumpeditha the custom was to submit to *haliṣah*. (*Otzar ha-Geonim, Yebamot,* responsa section, nos. 67–80). The countries of Europe were too varied in their customs, some practicing levirate marriage and others *haliṣah*. In the Sefardic communities of North Africa, and also of Yemen, Bavel, Persia and some of the Oriental communities that are in Israel even now, levirate marriage has priority over *haliṣah* (Introduction to Mishnah Yebamot, p. 10, by Albeck). Even while this is being published, between 1950 and 1960, things were changing as we shall describe later." (Introduction to Mishnah Yebamot, p. 10).

The reason for this variation in spite of the explicit statement in the Mishnah, is the following discussion in the Talmud: "We have learned elsewhere: At first, when the object was the fulfillment of the commandment, the precept of levirate marriage was preferable to that of *haliṣah;* now, however, when the object is not the fulfillment of the commandment, the precept of *haliṣah,* it was laid down, is preferable to that of levirate marriage. Said Rami B. Hama in the name of R. Isaac: It was reenacted that the precept of the levirate marriage is preferable to that of *haliṣah.*

Said R. Nahman b. Isaac to him: Have the generations improved in their morals?—at first they held the opinion of Abba Saul, and finally they adopted that of the rabbis. For it was taught: Abba Saul said "If a levir marries his sister-in-law on account of her beauty or in order to gratify his sexual desires or with any other ulterior motive, it is as if he has infringed upon the law of incest; and I am even inclined to think that the child of such union is a bastard." But the Sages said, "Her husband's brother shall go in unto her (Deuteronomy 25:5) whatever the motive" (B. Yebamot 39b).

Therefore, again, Maimonides, the Rashbam, and the Rabyah ruled that levirate marriage has priority; while Rabbenu Tam, Rabbenu Hananel, the Ravn, the Semag, (*Sefer mitzvot ha-gadol,* of Moses ben Jacob of Coucy) and other luminaries of France ruled that today *haliṣah* has priority (*Arukh ha-Shulhan, Eben ha-Ezer, Hilkhot Yibum,* 165:1-2)

Since most of the Sephardic communities are now in Israel, a new chapter is being written in the customs of these peoples. At least in this area the Ashkenazic practice is gaining ascendency.

In a case involving a levir who had a wife and children and who wanted to marry his brother's childless widow who objected to marrying him, the Court of Appeals (Bet Din Hagadol l'Irurim) ruled that though both were members of Sephardic communities which maintained that levirate marriage had priority, they should be instructed to submit to *halisah* rather than contract levirate marriage. This verdict was rendered 27 Sivan 5704.

A few years later it was extended further to cover all cases. At a national conference of the rabbis of Israel on the 18th to the 21st of Shevat 5710 the following resolution was passed: "We decree upon all who dwell in Israel and upon those who will come and settle in it henceforth, to forbid to them the performance of the commandment of levirate marriage, and they are obligated to submit to *halisah*. They are liable to the maintenance of the childless widow according to decision of the court until they will release her by means of *halisah*." (*Sefer ha-Agunot,* Kahana p. 62, A. H. Freiman, *Sinai,* vol. 14, pp. 258–260).

As of now the practice of levirate marriage is universally forbidden, and *halisah* has become the standard practice for K'lal Yisrael.

Let us now examine the status of the childless widow who is liable to *halisah*. There is the impression that she has the status of a married woman, the purpose of *halisah* being to release her from this bond she has to the levir just as a *get* releases a married woman from her marital ties. There are indications, however, that her status does not entirely parallel that of a married woman. If a married woman, for example, marries another man while legally still the wife of the first husband, even if she married the second man by error, the second marriage has no validity at all, and no formal act is necessary to release her from that marriage. In the case of the childless widow, however, if she married another man while awaiting levirate marriage, that marriage has enough validity to necessitate a *get* to dissolve it. (See B. Yebamot, 92b, and *Eben ha-Ezer* 159.1).

All this however, is of no help to us because the *get* in this case is merely an extra measure of severity and constitutes an additional burden on the widow rather than a means to mitigate her position, since under no circumstances is the marriage legitimate without *halisah*.

Another difference in the status of the childless widow is indicated by the rule that if she bears a child from another man while waiting for *haliṣa* or for levirate marriage, the child is not considered a bastard (ibid., 159:2) while if a married woman bears a child from another man the child is considered a bastard.

While all this clarifies the status of *haliṣah* and levirate marriage it does not help us to provide a remedy for a woman who comes to us for assistance nor point to any avenue for doing without *haliṣah* in cases of distress.

Thank the Lord—*Revah v'hatzala ya-amod layehudim mimakom aher*—a remedy can be found in instituting certain preventive measures—and there is ample precedent for such measures. In certain cases where *haliṣah* proved to be unfeasible, the authorities found ways to make it unnecessary. The classical case is that of the husband or the levir who becomes a *mumar,* an apostate. There is a difference of opinion between the geonim as to whether the wife is obligated in such cases to perform *haliṣah.* Rav Sherira Gaon maintains that as long as the levir is born a Jew she is obligated to perform *haliṣah* and may not marry until the apostate levir submits to *haliṣah* (Tur *Eben ha-Ezer* 157). Rav Yehudai Gaon qualified this decision by limiting the case to when the levir became an apostate after the brother's marriage. If he had become an apostate before his brother's marriage *haliṣah* was unnecessary (ibid). Rav Nahshon Gaon concurs (*Otzar ha-Geonim Yebamot* 36, 37). Of the earlier authorities Rashi has come out strongly against the opinion of Rav Yehudai Gaon and in favor of the opinion of Rav Sherira (See Bach on *Tur Eben ha-Ezer* 137 and in *Otzar haGeonim Yebamot* p. 37 note 1). All later authorities have followed the opinion of Rashi. Nevertheless, some later authorities dispensed with *haliṣah* in cases where the widow would become an *agunah* if *halisah* were insisted upon (See Sefer Ha-Agunoth, Kahana, p. 65).

All this still does not give us a remedy for the ordinary case of *halisah* where one of the parties refuses to cooperate or where circumstances militate against it.

In his gloss on *Eben ha-Ezer* 157:4, where R. Joseph Karo states his agreement with R. Sherira Gaon and Rashi, R. Moses Isserles, after quoting a number of opinions, presents the classic decision of R. Israel of Bruenn (1400–1480) which has become the basis of all later *takkanot* concerning women who are in distress because they are subject to *halisah*. "He who betrothes a woman and has a brother an apostate, he may betroth and stipulate with a double stipulation that should she become liable to the apostate brother for levirate marriage the betrothal should not become effective" (*Eben ha-Ezer* 157:4).

Rabbi Mordekhai Yaffe in his code, *Levush*, states even more explicitly: "If one who has an apostate brother betroths a woman, he may stipulate at the time of the betrothal with a double stipulation that if she should become liable for levirate marriage to the apostate the betrothal should become invalid retroactively. She is then exempt from levirate marriage and *halisah*. (*Levush, Eben ha-Ezer*, 157:4). This is evidently based on the *takkanah* of R. Israel of Bruen and became the accepted norm in the Ashkenazic communities. (*She-eilot u-Teshuvot Hayim Sha'al*, Part 2, No. 38, Sec. 68. *Sheilot u-Teshuvot Me'il Tzedakah* 1–4. See, however, in Meiri to Yebamot p. 57 to the contrary).

This *takkanah* was extended to include a deaf-mute levir (*Nahalat Shivah, Dinei Halisah* 22:8,) or when the levir has disappeared (see Bach, *Tur O.H.* 157; *She'eilot u-Teshuvot Shevut Ya'akov* Part 1, No. 127). The Bach has extended it to include cases when the levir has disappeared. Thus the Taz says: My father-in-law [Yoel Serkes —the Bach] of blessed memory wrote that the same law applies to one with a brother who had departed and there is no knowledge of whether he is still living, such a man may marry with the stipulation that should he die without children and there is no knowledge of the whereabouts of the brother who had departed that the betrothal be invalid. And it is permissible from the start to stipulate such a condition. Taz, *Eben ha-Ezer* 157 Sec 1). However, in *Shevut Ya'akov* Part 1, No. 127, the *takkanah* is limited to the case of an apostate. The Maharam Shick presents the case of one who had a brother in America which, in those days, was tantamount to a brother who had disappeared. There too the *takkanah* was applied (Maharam Shick, *Eben Ha-Ezer*, no. 70–72).

From some of the responsa it is evident that some authorities have made use of this *takkanah* generally (See *Sefer ha-Agunot*, p. 68, quoting *She'eilot u-Teshuvot Or Ne'elam* no. 30–31). Rabbi Selig Auerbach claims that this was the common usage in Hamburg. The suggestion was also made to Professor David Hoffman, but he rejected it for reasons that we shall mention later (See *Melamed l'Ho'il*, part 3, no. 5).

The implementation of this *takkanah* poses a number of difficulties. The first and most obvious is the principle that should one stipulate a condition that is contrary to the Torah the stipulation is null and void (B. Kiddushin 19b).

The authorities agree that the stipulation under consideration is not contrary to the Torah. The principle would apply where the stipulation is specifically to the effect that a law of the Torah should not apply, i.e., if the groom stipulates that he betrothes the woman on condition that if he dies without children the laws of levirate marriage should not apply. This is forbidden. Thus we have the statement in the Tosefta: If one says, Be thou betrothed to me on condition that you are not subject to levirate marriage, his condition is invalid (Tosefta Kiddushin 3:7; also P. Kiddushin 3:7).

In our case, the condition is that the marriage should become invalid retroactively. If the marriage is invalid, levirate marriage does not become necessary. That levirate marriage becomes unnecessary is merely a by-product (See Beth Shmuel Tur, *Eben ha-Ezer* 157 sub-sec. 6, *Arukh ha-Shulhan Eben ha-Ezer* 13:15).

The other problem is the principle of *ein tenai b'nisuin* (no condition may be stipulated in marriage B. Yebamot 107a). The controversy on this subject has created a whole literature. Its basic principle is that while the husband stipulates a condition at the time of the marriage, he is also liable to rescind that condition each time he cohabits with his wife. (For the latest, see *Noam VI*, pp. 1–69; Eliezer Berkovitz, *Tenai b'Nisuim u'b'Get*.

There is no doubt, however, that this rule is not absolute. The Bet Shmuel says, "Although we say generally that you cannot contract marriage conditionally, in a case like this, however, it was permitted." (*Eben ha-Ezer*, 157, *Beit Shmuel*, par. 6. See also ibid., in *Melamed l'Ho'il* Part 3, No. 31, and Rabbi E. Gershfield's paper on *Kiddushin al Tenai*, and, of course, Rabbi Louis Epstein's *Hatza'ah l'Takkanat Agunot*.)

The third objection is a psychological and sociologic one, and has been voiced by Professor David Hoffman. He is embarrassed at the taunts that will come from the direction of the reform groups who will say: See these rabbis who pose as the pious must admit the truth now, i.e., that their laws are not good, and what we have declared null and void in a straightforward manner because the spirit of times is against it, they come and declare null and void in an oblique and devious way. They have thereby admitted that the spirit of the times is stronger than these obsolete laws.—What can we answer to that? Is there a greater *hilul ha-Shem* than that? (*She'eilot u-Teshuvot Melamed l'Ho'il*, Part 3, No. 51)

While this fear is a real one and I can sympathize with it because it does sometimes give our halakhic discussions the aspect of a game and shadow play, I do not deem it a valid enough reason to refuse to find a remedy. As a matter of fact, in the very same responsum Professor Hoffman says: "We conclude from this that if the great rabbis of our time would join together to enact a *takkanah* to the effect that he who wishes may arrange a marriage with a condition attached, i.e., that should the husband die without leaving a viable child, and his brother will not submit to *halisah* within a whole year, and the rabbi of the city or of another place will write an attestation to his wife that it was beyond his power to make the levir submit to *halisah* until now, that the betrothal should be null and void" (ibid).

Evidently he felt that the taunt of Reform, by itself, is not enough reason to refuse such a *takkanah*. Surely the price is too high if, because of this apprehension, there should result even one *agunah*.

Thus we see a persistent effort to narrow the area of *halisah* almost to the point of total elimination. From the responsa that we quoted we gather from the way the questions were asked and instances cited that not only was there a desire to make *halisah* unnecessary when any difficulty is encountered, but that certain dayyanim actually made it a routine practice to stipulate at every marriage that should levirate marriage become necessary the marriage should become null and void retroactively. Rabbi Selig Auerbach as we mentioned before, claims that such was the practice of his native city, Hamburg.

To take the final step, that of eliminating *halisah* by attaching a condition before the marriage, is not so presumptuous any longer. It is therefore our suggestion that in cases of marriage where the wife may become liable for levirate marriage we should add to the *tenai* we already have, a clause that would include exemption from levirate marriage.

BIBLIOGRAPHY

She'eilot u-Teshuvot Noda b'Yehudah Kama Even Ha-ezer, No. 56

She'eilot u-Teshuvot Hatam Sofer Even ha-Ezer, Nos. 110, 111

She'eilot u-Teshuvot Shevut Ya'akov, No. 127

She'eilot u-Teshuvot Maharam Schik Eben ha-Ezer No. 70–72

She'eilot u-Teshuvot Melamed l'Ho'il, Part 3, No. 51

She'eilot u-Teshuvot Mishpetei Uziel, v. 2. No. 44

She'eilot u-Teshuvot Seridei Eish, Part 3 Nos. 25, 44, 117

Noam, v. 1 pp. 1–59; v. 6 p. 112

Nahalat Shivah, Dinei Shtar Halisah, No. 22

Arukh haShulhan, Even Ha-ezer, Hilkhot Yibum, 157:13–16

Sefer ha-Agunot, Kahana, pp. 64–71.

Tenai b'Nisuin Vb'get, Eliezer Berkowitz, pp. 29–51

Seder Kiddushin V'nisuin, A. H. Freiman, 386–388

3. THE MARRIAGE OF A KOHEN TO A GIYORET (1968)

QUESTION : *May a rabbi officiate at a marriage between a* kohen *and a* giyoret?

ANSWER: In the 1954 *Proceedings of the Rabbinical Assembly* there is a responsum on the question of whether a rabbi may officiate at a marriage between a *kohen* and a *gerusha*. It would seem at first glance that the answer given there would also apply to our question, but after further consideration it has become apparent that this is quite a different question and that other factors are involved.

Sources: The laws prescribing which women a *kohen* may marry are based on the biblical verse: "They shall not take a woman that is a harlot or profaned, nor shall they marry a woman divorced from her husband" (Leviticus 21:7). The Bible itself explains the reason for these restrictions: ". . . for he is holy unto his God" (ibid).

Definition of Terms: Halalah, which we translated as a profane woman, refers to the daughter of a forbidden marriage contracted by a *kohen,* as, for example, the daughter of a high priest (*kohen gadol*) married to a widow, or a woman who had already entered into a forbidden marriage to a *kohen* (B. Kiddushin 77a).

Zonah, which we translated as a harlot, is expanded by the rabbis of the Talmud to include all women whose moral purity is impugned. Thus the Talmud says: "*Zonah* refers solely to a *giyoret,* an emancipated bondswoman, and a woman who had illicit intercourse, i.e., a harlot" (B. Yebamot 61b). Female proselytes were therefore considered as women with a past who were unfit to become the wife of a *kohen.*

In the Talmud there is a difference of opinion as to how far these restrictions apply. One opinion is that they apply only to proselytes who were converted when they were over three years old. Thus the Talmud says: "Rabbi Simeon ben Yohai says: A female proselyte less than three years and one day old is eligible to

22

marry a *kohen*" (B. Kiddushin 78a, Yebamot 60b). The majority opinion is that we do not make this distinction and exclude all proselytes. According to some opinions it even applies to the children of female proselytes (Mishnah, Bikkurim 1:5, Kiddushin 4:6, 7).

The Talmud explains that these differing opinions are based upon conflicting interpretations given to the verse in the Prophet Ezekiel that contains the regulations concerning women who are eligible for marriage to a *kohen*. The verse reads: They shall not marry a widow, or a divorced woman, but only a vergin of the stock of the house of Israel, or a widow who is the widow of a priest (Ezekiel 44:22).

These regulations in the Book of Ezekiel obviously differ in many respects from those in the Book of Leviticus, and led the Talmud to make what we consider to be forced interpretations of the text of the Book of Ezekiel.

The relevant words concerning our question are "but only a virgin of the stock of the house of Israel." These are given varying interpretations so that they may serve as support for the four opinions we mentioned above.

We thus have two sources for the law that a *kohen* may not marry a *giyoret*. One is the verse in the Book of Leviticus as interpreted by the rabbis, i.e., that *zonah* refers to a *giyoret*. The other is the regulation in the Book of Ezekiel prescribing that a *kohen* may marry only a woman "of the stock of the house of Israel."

Maimonides rules: "We have learned by tradition that the term 'harlot' as designated in the Torah means any woman who is not a daughter of Israel (Mishneh Torah Laws Concerning Forbidden Marriages 18:1). He thus bases the interdict against such a marriage on the verse in Leviticus. According to the stricture of the RABD this interdict is based on the verse in Ezekiel that makes it obligatory for the *kohen* to marry only a daughter of Israel—which excludes a proselyte (ibid).

Some commentators combine the two by saying that whosoever is not a *bat Yisroel* ("a daughter of Israel") is *b'heskat zonah* ("presumed to be a harlot") (See *Yad Halevy* on Sefer Hamitsvot of Maimonides, and also *Rambam l'Am* on *Sefer Hamitsvot*, Negative Commandment 158; also *Tosafot* on B. Yebamot 61a, s.v., *V' ein Zonah elah giyoret;* also *Torah Temimah* on Leviticus 21:7).

Whatever the reason, the accepted law has been that a *kohen* may not marry a *giyoret* (*Eben Ha-Ezer* 6:8).

Attitude Towards Proselytes

While the talmudic tradition is not in favor of proselytizing, it nevertheless considered the proselyte most worthy of love, appreciation, and endearment. Again and again it is stressed that the proselyte is equal in every respect to a born Israelite. Practically the only exception is the case of marriage to a *kohen*. Since the Rabbinical Assembly has permitted a rabbi to officiate at a wedding between a *kohen* and a divorced woman we would assume that the same permission would apply to the wedding between a *kohen* and a *giyoret* (See *Rabbinical Assembly Proceedings* 1954 pp. 55–61). Upon careful reflection we came to the conclusion that there is an additional consideration here. In the case of a divorced woman the reason for the prohibition is that she is a *"pegumah"* (marred woman) without prejudice to her status otherwise. In the case of a *giyoret,* however, she is stamped as harlot, which is a greater stigma than a *pegumah*. Most of the authorities maintain that even when the individual woman is not suspected of immorality, as for example when she is still an infant, she nevertheless has the status of a harlot because her people are *sh'tufim b'zimah* ("steeped in immorality"). Maimonides makes an effort to blunt the sharpness of the term and equates it with *"pegumah"* (see Mishnah Torah, Laws Concerning Forbidden Marriages 18:5, and note 1 thereto in the Yale Judaica Series). Most other authorities, however, allow the term to stand for what it usually represents. This being the case, a new factor enters here, the element of *hilul ha-Shem* (desecration of the Name).

In studying the question I have come across two cases that are relevant and that can serve as precedents. One is the case of a *kohen* who was married in a civil ceremony to a non-Jewish woman. A child was born of this marriage and was circumcised. Later the woman was moved to adopt the faith of her child. She was so anxious to do this that a refusal, it was feared, might endanger her mental health.

The question was presented to the renowned Professor David Hoffman. He answered that they should convert her, and gave the following reason: Although there is a prohibition against a *kohen* marrying a *giyoret*, there is a greater *issur* ("prohibition") against living with a non-Jewish wife. Furthermore, there is the threat of a *hillul ha-Shem* if we should refuse to convert her. Should our refusal to convert her result in suffering, we would be accused of not showing compassion to a non-Jew (*Responsa,* Melamed l'Ho'il v. 3, responsum 8).

The other took place in Bulgaria. A non-Jewish girl fell in love with a Jew and was converted to Judaism in order to become eligible to marry him. When they were about to be married, the officiating rabbi discovered that the groom was a *kohen* and therefore refused to marry the couple. This resulted in bitterness on the part of the young man and anti-Jewish anger on the part of the non-Jewish population.

The problem was brought before Rabbi Yehudah Leib Zirlsohn, rabbi of Kishinev. He permitted the marriage because of the disturbed situation that was fraught with such danger to the Jewish community as a result of the refusal, and in order to prevent further *hillul ha-Shem*. The only *caveat* was that this was not to be considered a precedent for future decisions (She'eilot u-Teshuvot Ma'arkhei Lev, Responsa 72).

It is our considered opinion that in our day there could not be a graver *hillul ha-Shem* than to declare that such a marriage is forbidden because the female proselytes are deemed to have the status of harlots because their people, even if not they themselves, were *shetufim b'zimah*. If the rabbis of the Talmud considered the heathens of their day as *shetufim b'zimah* because of the high standard of morality of the children of Israel in their day, can we make such a distinction between Jew and non-Jew today? Neither situation obtains today. The non-Jews are not *shetufim bezimah* and the children of Israel are not as pure morally as they used to be. *V'dayah L'hakimah.* . . .

In Israel, where the rabbinate will not officiate at such a wedding, some people have taken matters into their own hands. Since such a marriage is legally valid because *kidushin tofsin* ("the marriage act takes effect") and the only obstacle is that the official rabbis refuse to officiate at such a wedding, and since traditional Jewish law does not require the presence of a rabbi, they arrange that the *kidushin* should take place in the presence of two witnesses without a rabbi. Legally, the rabbinic courts have to recognize such a marriage and are left with a most embarrassing situation. There is legislation pending in Israel regarding such marriages. (See Dykan, *Dinei Nisu-in v'Geirushin*, p. 196; *Osef Piskei Din shel Ha-rabbanut Ha-rashit*, Jerusalem, 5710, pp. 132–139; *Ha-Peraklit*, February 1954, p. 82, 85; June 1954, p. 107.)

Other Consideration

In these cases we should also take into consideration the opinion that the status of *kohanim* today is in doubt (*sh'ein mahzikim oto k'kohen vadai;* O. H. Sec. 457, in *Magen Avraham* Sub-sec. 109).

Furthermore, while the non-Jews of today do have the status of the *akum* of the Talmud, they are on par with the children of Israel in many respects. (See Encyclopedia Talmudit, under *goy*) In this category we would like to include the question of *shetufim bezimah*, although this was not done so explicitly in the past.

In view of all the foregoing considerations, it is our considered opinion that a rabbi should be permitted to officiate at a wedding between a *kohen* and *giyoret*.

BIBLIOGRAPHY

Ginsberg, Louis, *Geonica*, v. 2. p. 394.
Hildesheimer, Azriel, *Halakhot Gedolot* Sec. 14.
Otzar ha-Geonim, Yebamot p. 139
Minhat Hinukh, sec. 267, Os Aleph
Otzar ha-Posekim, v. 1., *Eben ha-Ezer* 6:8
She'eilot u-Teshuvot Melamed L'ho'il, Part 3, responsum 8
She'eilot u-Teshuvot Igrot Mosheh, *Eben ha-Ezer* Sec. 11
She'eilot u-Techuvot Ma-arkhei Lev, R. Yehudah Leib Zirlsohn, responsum 72
She'eliot u-Teshuvot Heikhal Yitzhak, R. Isaac Halevy Herzog, v. 1, responsum 16
Encyclopedai Talmudit, under "Giyoret"
B. Kiddushin 77a; Yebamot 61b, 60b
Maimonides, Laws Concerning Forbidden Marriages 18:1
Eben ha-Ezer 6:8

4. ABORTION (1959)

QUESTION: *Is abortion permitted according to Jewish law?*

ANSWER: Before answering this question, we must first define the word "abortion." Medically, an abortion is the spontaneous or artificial termination of a pregnancy before the twenty-eighth week of pregnancy, at which time the infant, theoretically, first becomes able to carry on an independent existence. (*The Management of Obstetric Difficulties* by Titus and Wilson, 1955, p. 210.) In our case the question applies only to the artificial, not the spontaneous or natural termination of the pregnancy at any time before the complete birth of the child and involving the death of the embryo or the foetus.

The main talmudic source for this question is to be found in the Mishnah:

> If a woman is having difficulty giving birth, it is permitted to cut up the child inside her womb and take it out limb by limb because her life takes precedence. If the greater part of the child has come out it must not be touched, because one life must not be taken to save another (Ahalot 7:6).

This is repeated in the Tosefta with slight variations:

> If a woman is having difficulty giving birth, it is permitted to cut up the child in her womb even on the Sabbath, and take it out limb by limb because her life takes precedence. If its head has come out it may not be touched even on the second day, because one life may not be taken to save another (Tosefta Yebamot 9:4).

On the above Mishnah we have the following comment of the Talmud:

> "Once his head has come forth he may not be harmed because one life may not be taken to save another." But why so? Is he not a pursuer? There, it is different, for she is pursued by heaven (B. Sanhedrin 72b).

27

What is the reason that we permit taking the life of the unborn child when it endangers the life of the mother? Rashi in his comment on the above passage gives the following reason:

> For as long as it did not come out into the world it is not called a living thing and it is permissible to take its life in order to save its mother. Once the head has come forth it may not be harmed because it is considered born, and one life may not be taken to save another.

Thus, according to Rashi, the reason that it is permitted to take the life of the unborn child is that the embryo is not considered a living thing and, hence, taking its life cannot be called murder.

This view is supported by biblical law concerning any harm done to a pregnant woman in which case the Bible prescribes:

> If men strive and hurt a woman with child so that her fruit depart from her and yet no mischief follow: he shall surely be punished, according as the woman's husband will lay upon him; and he shall pay as the judge determine. And if any mischief follow, then thou shalt give life for life (Exodus 21:22–23).

The mischief in the verse refers, of course, to the death of the woman. It is only if death to the mother results from the hurt that capital punishment follows. The death of the unborn child is punishable by fine only.

From Maimonides it would appear that the reason the life of the unborn child may be taken when it endangers the life of the mother is based on the law of the "pursuer," *rodeph*. In his code Maimonides says:

> This is, moreover, a negative commandment, that we have no pity on the life of a pursuer. Consequently, the sages have ruled that if a woman with child is having difficulty in giving birth, the child inside her may be taken out, either by drugs or by surgery, because it is regarded as one pursuing her and trying to kill her. But once its head has appeared, it must not be touched, for we may not set aside one human life to save another human life, and what is happening is the course of nature (code of Maimonides, Murder and the Preservation of Life, 1:9).

This opinion of Maimonides is followed by Joseph Karo in the *Hoshen Mishpat* (425:2).

There is, then, a clear distinction between the reasoning of Rashi and that of Maimonides. According to Rashi, the embryo is not considered a living being and therefore the life of the mother takes precedence. According to Maimonides, the life of the mother takes precedence because the embryo is in the position of a *rodeph*, a "pursuer."

From this difference in interpretation may also result differences in legal decisions. According to Maimonides, we should permit abortion only where there is clear danger to the life of the mother. According to Rashi, there might be other adequate reasons beside the threat to the life of the mother.

Maimonides' interpretation offers many difficulties. There is no indication in the Mishnah that in the case of an embryo the law of the pursuer applies. On the contrary, the Mishnah clearly states that the life of the mother takes precedence as long as the child is unborn. The Talmud suggests using the reason of the "pursuer" only when the child is already born. The answer that the Talmud gives for not applying the reason of the "pursuer" in the case of a child already born applies just as much to the unborn child. Many of the commentators try to give answers, but they all seem forced. (See Tosafot R. Akiba Eiger on the Mishnah in Ahalot, and Hidushei R. Hayin Halevi ad loc. and comments in some of the responsa that deal with this question.) Hence we prefer to follow the reasoning of Rashi that the whole problem revolves around the question of whether the foetus is considered a living being.

The ancients spoke of this in their idiom. The following conversation took place between the compiler of the Mishnah and the Roman emperor:

> Antoninus said to Rabbi: When is the soul given unto man, at the time that the embryo is formed, or at the time of conception? He replied, at the time the embryo is already formed. The emperor objected: Is it possible for a piece of meat to stay for three days without salt and not putrify? It must therefore be at conception. Said Rabbi: This thing Antoninus taught me and Scripture supports him, as it is said; And thy providence has preserved my spirit [my soul] (Job 10:12).

According to Aristotle the rational soul is infused on the fortieth day after conception in the case of a male and on the eightieth day in the case of a female. The Platonic tradition was that the soul entered at conception. The Stoics believed that the soul entered at birth. Roman jurists followed the Stoics and held therefore that abortion was not murder. According to common law, too, taking a life is punishable only after there has been complete extrusion of the child from the body of the mother.

The Catholic church evidently followed the Platonic tradition because it forbade all abortions. Even in the case of ectopic pregnancies the official ruling of the church issued by the Congregation of the Holy Office, March, 1902 is: No, it [abortion] is not lawful. Such a removal of the foetus is a direct killing of the foetus and is forbidden.

A *fatwa* of the Grand Mufti of January 25th, 1937, states that therapeutic abortions are absolutely forbidden after the embryo has "quickened." Medical science considers the foetus a living thing from the moment the ovum is fertilized. (See *Obstetrics*, Joseph B. De Lee, 4th edition, p. 274.)

Actually being a living thing and being a separate entity are two separate matters. Even if the foetus is a living thing we can say that it is *pars viscera matrum*, or to use the talmudic expression, *ubar yerah emo hu*, the foetus is accounted as the loin of its mother. When abortion is therapeutic there can be no objection to it because, as in any surgery, we sacrifice the part for the whole.

This is the attitude the rabbis have taken: Abortion is forbidden. Although it is not considered murder, it does mean the destruction of potential life. (See Tosafot, B. Hulin 33a, s.v., Ehad Akum) If, however, the purpose is therapeutic, this objection is removed. I have chosen a number of responsa dealing with the question.

Rabbi Yair Hayyim Bachrach (1639–1702), the author of *Responsa, Havot Ya'ir*, describes this strange case. A married woman committed adultery and became pregnant. She had pangs of remorse and wanted to do penance. She asked whether she could swallow a drug in order to get rid of the "evil fruit" in her womb.

In answer, Rabbi Bachrach made it clear immediately that the question of the permissibility of abortion has nothing to do with the legitimacy of the child to be born. The only question involved is whether abortion is to be accounted as taking a life or not. Rabbi

Bachrach draws distinctions between the various stages of the development of the foetus, i.e., forty days after conception, three months after conception, then he concludes that theoretically an abortion might be permitted at the early stages of the pregnancy, but we do not do so because of the custom adopted both by the Jewish and the general community against immorality.

Rabbi Meir Eisenstadt (1670–1744) in his *Panim me-irot* asks the following question: If a woman has difficulty in giving birth because the child came out feet first, is it permitted to cut up the child limb by limb in order to save the mother?

This seems to be the very question explicitly answered in the Mishnah. The only problem that is introduced is a discrepancy between the Mishnah and Maimonides. Whereas the Mishnah states that if the greater part of the child has come out of the mother's body we do not take the life of the child in order to save the mother, Maimonides says that if the head of the child or the majority thereof came out it is considered as born and we do not take its life in order to save the mother.

The commentators tried to resolve this contradiction by claiming that the extrusion of the head or the major part of the head or, in cases when the head came last, the extrusion of the majority of the body, constitutes birth.

The author then poses the question: If at this stage death could result to both should we let nature take its course, is it still forbidden to take the life of the child in order to save the mother? He leaves the question unanswered. (See, however, *Melamed l'Ho'il* v. 2., responsum 69.)

Rabbi Eliezer Deutsch (1850–1916), the author of *Responsa, Peri Hasadeh,* treats the following problem: A woman who has been pregnant for a few weeks began to spit blood. Physicians insisted that she must take a drug to induce a miscarriage for, should she wait, it would not only become necessary to take out the child by cutting it up, it would also endanger the life of the mother; if they acted immediately, it would be possible to bring forth the child with a drug. Is it permissible to do so?

Rabbi Deutsch answers that in this case it is certainly permitted. He also makes a distinction between the various stages in the development of the foetus, *gufa aharina* ("a separate body"), *ne-ekar ha-vlad* ("the foetus has become detached"), between the use of drugs and the use of surgery, and between another person performing the abortion or the woman herself. The conclusion is that it is permitted in this case for three reasons: (a) Before three months after conception there is not even a foetus. (b) There is no overt act involved in this case (i.e. surgery). (c) The woman herself is doing it and it is thus an act of self-preservation.

In current literature I found a responsum dated 5709—*I, Hayei Sara* by Rabbi Yitzchack Oelbaum of Czechoslovakia, now of Canada. This is the question: A woman has a weak child. According to the doctors it will not live unless it is breast fed by the mother. The mother has been pregnant for four weeks and has felt a change in her milk. Could she destroy the child she is carrying by means of an injection, she inquired, in order to save the child she is nursing.

The author discusses the reliability of doctors in these things, claiming that they sometimes exaggerate, and whether a proper formula for bottle-feeding could be substituted. He concludes that if there is expert evidence that danger might result if the abortion is not performed, then it is permitted.

In this responsum a new issue is introduced. Until now, we have spoken of danger to the mother, but here there is no danger to the mother but rather to another child. This opens new possibilities which, however, we shall not pursue here.

An even more recent responsum on the subject is by Rabbi Gedaliah Felder of Toronto, published in the current issue of *Kol Torah*, a rabbinic periodical published in Jerusalem. The question is: A pregnant woman is afflicted with cancer of the lungs. The doctors say that if a premature birth will not be effected, the cancer will spread faster and hasten her death. Is it permissible to have an abortion where the mother can be saved only temporarily? (*Kol Torah*, Heshvan 5719)

Before we sum up, it would not be out of place to present a comment from the medical profession. This was called to my attention by Dr. Hiram Yellen, a most prominent obstetrician of the city of Buffalo.

There is abundant evidence that the frequency of criminal induction of abortion is increasing at an alarming rate, although accurate statistics cannot be obtained. Numerous reasons may be advanced for this deplorable situation, the most probable being: (1) Twentieth-century standards of living have made children an economic liability for a large percentage of the population. This may be contrasted with more primitive rural conditions where a large family was considered an economic asset. (2) As a by-product of the woman's freedom movement, a very large number of women have come to believe that pregnancy should be regulated by their personal desires. (3) The present-day lack of religious feeling and the wide teaching that pregnancy may be controlled have contributed to a lowering of moral standards among women, with a resulting increase in the number of undesired pregnancies. . . ." (*Gynecology and Obstetrics,* by Carl Henry Davis, 1937 chapt. x, p. 1).

Our conclusion, therefore, must be that abortion is morally wrong. It should be permitted only for therapeutic reasons.

BIBLIOGRAPHY

Mishnah Ahalot 7:6 and *Tosafot Rabbi Akiba Eger* thereto; Tosefta Yebamot 9:4

B. Sanhedrin 72b, 91b

Tosafot on B. Hulin 33a, s.v., *Ehad Akum*

Maimonides, Laws Concerning Murder and Preservation of Life, 1:9

Karo, *Hoshen Mishpat* 452:2

She-eilot u-Teshuvot Panim Me'irot, part 3, no. 8

She-eilot u-Teshuvot Havot Ya'ir, no. 31

She-eilot u-Teshuvot Peri ha-Sadeh, part 4, no. 50

She-eilot u-Teshuvot Maharam Shick, *Yoreh De'ah,* no. 155

She-eilot u-Teshuvot Melamed l'Ho-il, part 2, no. 69

She-eilot u-Teshuvot She-eilat Yitshak, no. 64

Kol Torah, Heshvan 5719

Harofeh ha-Ivri, 1953, p. 124

Fletcher, *Morals and Medicine*

5. AUTOPSY (1958)

QUESTION: *Is autopsy permitted according to Halakhah?*

ANSWER: There is a whole literature around this question because it involves a number of problems posed by developments in the medical field. It involves the use of bodies for dissection in medical schools. It involves the transplanting of tissues from a deceased into a living body as well as post-mortem examinations performed to study a disease with the purpose of furthering medical knowledge (i.e., to ascertain the exact manifestations of the disease from which the deceased died with a view to more efficient treatment of other cases of the same disease), or for juridical purposes (i.e., when there is suspicion of crime, to ascertain from the condition of the body, particularly the internal organs, whether or not death was due to natural causes.)

The first recorded instance of this question in the form of a formal responsum comes to us from Ezekiel Landau (1713–1793) in responsum 210 *Noda b'Yehuda Tinyana* on *Yoreh De'ah*. It treats a specific case of a man who was operated on in London for gallstones and died. The doctors wanted permission for an autopsy in order to improve techniques for future cases.

The answer of the *Noda b'Yehuda* is as follows:

> The principle that even a possibility [not a certainty—I. K.] of saving a life waives all biblical commandments except in three cases applies only when such a possibility is concretely before us, as, for instance, a person who is sick with that same ailment. In our case, however, there is no patient whose treatment calls for this knowledge. It is only that people want to learn this skill in case of a future possibility that a patient will come before us who will need this treatment. For such a slight apprehension we do not nullify a biblical commandment or even a rabbinic prohibition.

What is this biblical commandment that Rabbi Eziekiel Landau speaks about? The rabbis saw in the following biblical prescription an injunction for the reverent treatment of the body or the prohibition of *nivul ha-met*, ("dishonoring the dead").

34

And if a man have committed a sin worthy of death, and he be put to death, and thou hang him on a tree; his body shall not remain all night upon the tree, but thou shalt surely bury him the same day (Deuteronomy 21:22–23).

In the Talmud, there are a number of places where the prohibition against *nivul hamet* is implied. These are the most explicit ones:

It once happened at Bene-Berak that a person sold his father's estate, and died. The members of the family, thereupon, protested that he was a minor at the time of his death. They came to Rabbi Akiba and asked whether the body might be exhumed. He replied to them: You are not permitted to dishonor him (*l'navlo*). (B. Baba Bathra 154a).

Whence do we learn the principle that we follow the majority? Said Rav Kahana: I learn it from the case of one who commits murder for which the Torah prescribes the penalty of death. Why don't we suspect that the person murdered might have been *traif* (i.e. but rather assume that he was physically normal like most people)? Should you say that we examine the body in order to ascertain whether it has a blemish that would make the man *treif?* That would mean dishonoring the body (by dissection which is forbidden) (B. Hulin 11b).

Upon these statements in the Talmud the rabbis have based their objection to any disfiguring of the body of the deceased.

Rabbi Moses Sofer (Hatam Sofer) (1763–1839) in responsum 336 in *Yoreh De'ah* comes to the same conclusion as Rabbi Ezekiel Landau. To those who would want to permit dissections on the grounds of *pikuah nefesh* ("saving of lives") which supersedes all prohibitions, he says that this applies only where there is a person with the same disease present who would benefit from an autopsy on a person who died from this disease.

It is obvious that in spite of the great halakhic prestige and competence of these two authorities the matter could not rest there. With the pressure from medical schools who wanted bodies for dissection as well as the urgency of physicians who had special cases, the question came up again and again. In a number of European medical schools it became an issue upon which depended whether Jewish candidates would be accepted in medical schools. In a number of Jewish communities, as a result, the policy was adopted to permit such dissections. (See, *Universal Jewish Encyclopedia* under Autopsy.)

In America, the request to permit autopsies came from the Denver Hospital in order to study tuberculosis. The question is recorded in *Yagdil Torah*, a rabbinic monthly (5676–77) p. 3. Rabbi Eliezer Meir Prail and Dr. Bernard Revel reaffirm the position of the previous authorities. With much scholarship and *pilpul* they come to the same conclusion. There is only one dissenting voice that sounds a new note. It is from Rabbi Yehudah Leib Levin of Detroit. He says:

> However, in order not to shut the door to medical progress, and Scripture says "Her ways are ways of pleasantness," I am inclined to think if a patient has, while alive, consented fully and with a legal validation, then it is permissible to dissect him (*Yagdil Torah*, p. 112).

The general opinion, however, is expressed forcefully by Rabbi Prail whose answer is also reprinted in his collection of responsa, *Sefer Hama'or*, responsa 37–41. He says:

> With this we started and with this we end, that it is forbidden to dissect the dead bodies of Jews for the purpose of learning the nature of the disease even if there are sick people present who need this, because the cure is not clearly known. And even when the cure is clear, nevertheless, according to Rashi and Mei'ri, it is forbidden since one is not permitted to save himself by causing a loss to others. . . . If because of the autopsy the body of the dead will be kept overnight, there is the additional transgression of *halanat ha-met*, keeping the dead overnight. It is certainly forbidden for a physician who is a kohen to do the autopsy because there is the *issur* of *tumat Kohen*, the interdict against the defilement of a kohen (*Yagdil Torah*, 8th year, p. 57).

This, of course, goes beyond the decisions of the Hatam Sofer who permits an autopsy when there are sick people present who could benefit by it. Furthermore, the distinction of Rabbi Prail between a sure cure and one that is not sure is surprising. How can one know the cure before trying it? (See strictures of Rabbi Nasan Nateh Hurewitz, *Yagdil Torah*, 87.)

Rabbi Prail has softened his hard decision only in one instance.

He says:

> Accordingly, it is possible to say that if the patients and
> their relatives waive their privilege of the reverence due to
> dead bodies and consent to the performance of an autopsy, it
> is permitted. It is only when it is done against their wishes
> that it is forbidden.

Rabbi Prail adds an explanation in parentheses that the position
of the Hatam Sofer that one is forbidden to sell his body to a physician in order to be dissected after his death is explained on the basis
of the *issur hana'ah*, the interdiction against deriving any benefit
from a dead body. If he does not take money for it this cannot apply. However, evidently Rabbi Prail is himself surprised at this
liberal attitude and therefore adds immediately:

> However, even in this fashion it is forbidden to do so be-
> cause of dishonoring the dead, for if this person pays no
> attention to his own honor he certainly does not pay honor to
> his Maker as the Hatam Sofer mentioned (See also *Sefer
> Hama'or*, p. 179).

The question is approached in an entirely different vein by Rabbi
Chayim Hirshenson. He devotes a chapter to it in the third part of
his celebrated work *Malkie Bakodesh*. It is actually a refutation of
the strict view of Rabbis Prail and Revel. While the latter simply
rehashed the responsa of the *Noda b'Yehudah* and the *Hatam Sofer*,
Rabbi Hirshenson goes back to the sources. First he defines what
we mean by *nivul ha-met*. We usually interpret it as mutilation.
That in itself, however, is not *nivul*. The term applies to an act in-
flicted upon the dead that will dishonor the living and also do dishonor to the soul of the deceased rather than to his body. The term
bizayon ha-met can thus apply only to cases where that was the
intention. Where these things are done *l'kavod ha-met* there is no
nivul. Thus the Talmud says:

> If he kept him overnight for the sake of his honor, to pro-
> cure him a coffin or a shroud, he does not transgress thereby ...
> (Sanhedrin 47a).
> When did the Merciful One say, His body shall not remain
> all night upon the tree—only in a case similar to the hanged,
> where it involves disgrace. Nothing that is done for the honor
> of the living involves dishonor to the dead (B. Sanhedrin 47a).

Rabbi Hirshenson concludes, therefore, that in cases where physicians are seeking a cure for a disease and they think that through an autopsy they might find its cause and bring help to humanity, in general, and to those sick who are waiting for a cure, in particular, an autopsy should be permitted.

However, this does not apply to the use of bodies for dissection in medical schools. There Rabbi Hirshenson maintains there is no *kavod ha-hayim* nor *tsoreh ha-hayim* inasmuch as there are condemned criminals that are available and their use for dissection is permitted.

Rabbi Ben Zion Uziel, the late chief rabbi of the Sephardic community of Israel, went even further than Rabbi Hirshenson. From two talmudic sources he proves that where even *piku'ah nefesh* or loss of money is involved, there is no *issur nivul ha-met*. It is only a dishonor to the dead when an act is committed for that purpose. Autopsy, therefore, where the body is dissected either to learn medicine or to heal other people, is perfectly permissible. To the objection of the Hatam Sofer that *piku'ah nefesh* is only where one with such a disease is present, Rabbi Uziel answers that there must be other people with that disease even if they are not present and concludes, therefore, that both autopsies and dissections made for purposes of study are permitted. However, this applies only where there is no compensation to the person while alive or to his heirs for the use of his body. That would certainly be *bizayon ha-met*.

There are two qualifications that Rabbi Uziel adds. One is that after the body has been cut up all the remains should be given proper burial. The second is that all this *l'halakhah v'lo l'ma'aseh*. For the practical decision the question will have to be presented to the chief rabbinate.

Evidently the question was not long in coming. When the Hadassah University Hospital was established, it entered into a formal agreement with the chief rabbinate part of the text of which is as follows:

> Concordat Entered between the Chief Rabbinate of
> Israel and the Hadassah University Hospital.
> 1. 1. The Chief Rabbinate does not interfere with autopsies
> in the following categories:
>   a. Autopsies according to the requirements of law (to
>   ascertain foul play).

b. Cases in which the physician, because of lack of knowledge, cannot ascribe to any disease the cause of death without surgical operation (autopsy). Permission for such autopsy to be given on condition that a certificate, according to the attached form, will certify that there is no possibility whatsoever to establish a cause of death without autopsy. This certificate shall be given and signed by the three doctors after a consultation among themselves: (1) the doctor in whose ward the patient died, or in his absence, the resident of the hospital; (2) director of the hospital, and in his absence, his substitute; (3) director of the institute for anatomy and histologic pathology; in his absence his substitute.

c. Autopsy to save a life. In this category is included only such cases where an autopsy may be of help to a patient at that time in the hospital or outside it.

d. In cases of hereditary diseases when there is a necessity to guide the family in its care. In these cases of experimentation there shall be a consultation with the Rabbinnate.

2. In addition to the certificate of the three doctors, the hospital shall have a chart, in accordance with the attached form, that shall show under which category the autopsy was made on the deceased. In those cases where secrecy is not deemed necessary, the disease shall be recorded. The hospital administration shall provide a copy to the Hevra Kadisha (Ritual Burial Society) and a copy to the Religious Council of the Jerusalem Communities, the Knesset Israel.

3. The hospital administration shall endeavor to submit a copy to Hevra Kadisha or to notify them by telephone about the outcome of the autopsy as early as possible before the funeral.

4. The hospital administration takes upon itself to carry out the autopsy in a way befitting the honor of the deceased.

5. The organs that shall be removed from the body for medical inspection, either microscopic or otherwise, that shall be deemed necessary by the Institute of Anatomy and Histological Pathology to ascertain the cause of death, shall remain in the Institute as long as necessary. At the conclusion of the investigation the organs shall be turned over to the Hevra Kadisha for burial, and the hospital is to bear the expense of burial.

This concordat mentions only autopsies, but not the use of bodies in medical schools.

The question of whether a person can will his body to be used for the purpose of grafting parts of it into a living person in order to effect certain cures involves the same principles as does the question of autopsy and the transplanting of an eye. (The transplanting of an eye has been permitted by various rabbinic bodies.)

The objection in those cases stems from two principles:

1. *Nivul ha-met* ("disgracing the dead body") ;
2. *Issur hana'ah min ha-met* ("the interdict against deriving any benefit from the dead body").

The consensus of opinion is that if there is *pikuah nefesh,* the *issur nivul ha-met* does not apply. We can summarize it in the words of Rabbi Uziel:

It is reasonable that we call *nivul* only when done to dishonor the dead or where it is of no help to others (v. 1, p. 209).

The question of *issur hana'ah* does not apply here. There is the talmudic law: "One may cure himself with everything except three things" (B. Pesahim 43a). The *issur hana'ah* would refer only to making a business out of it—i.e., to sell oneself for that purpose. See responsum *Rabbinical Council of America Proceedings,* 1948, p. 50) The question of *kevurah* ("burial") has already been covered in the concordat between the Chief Rabbinate and the Hadassah University Hospital. We should add that the care insisted upon in the case of the organs applies to the blood, too. That too needs *kevurah.*

There is, however, the further question of a person who wills his body so that each part of it can be used for transplantation. This would eliminate burial altogether. There is the question of law and there is the question of sentiment and the entire procedure that centers around *kevurah.*

According to the Talmud, burial is a biblical commandment. "Rabbi Yohanan said in the name of Rabbi Simon ben Yochai: Where is there an indication in the Torah that burial is obligatory? In the verse, Thou shalt not bury him" (B. Sanhedrin 46b).

The Talmud also takes into consideration the feelings of the family and the sentiments of the person now dead. Thus, if an insult to the family results therefrom his request is not to be considered. The Talmud does not come to any decision. Later *posekim* have taken the line that *bizayon* is decisive.

> The students asked: Is burial in order to avert disgrace (*Tosafot*: "to the family") or as a means of atonement? What is the practical difference? If one said, 'I do not wish to be buried.' If the reason for burial is to avert disgrace to the family, he has no right to make such a request; if it is for atonement, then he has in effect declared, 'I do not desire atonement' (B. Sanhedrin 46b).

Today we should follow the same line of reasoning. Since the use of parts of the body is permissible and the only question is the elimination of *kevurah*, we should take into consideration the feelings of the next of kin. If they give their consent to such a bequest, we should honor it.

I would like to add an interesting comment in Responsa, *Havalim Banimim*, v. 3, sec. 64. He says:

> In a country where the Jews enjoy freedom, if the rabbis should refuse to allow the Jewish dead to be used for medical study, their action will result in Hillul ha-Shem, for it will be said that the Jews are not interested in saving lives; there is reason to permit it.

A similar opinion is to be found, *Atzei Zeitim, Yoreh De'ah*, 60, that where there is a *hashash nezek l'yisroel*, we should permit it.

With this kind of reasoning, which is to be commended for its realism, we can permit all these uses of the bodies of the deceased where there is an obvious help to other people and where the general public considers such uses as *pikuah nefesh*. If medical science claims that these may save lives, then we should add that in such cases it is not only permitted, but is actually a *mitzvah*. There should always, however, be a respectful attitude to the human body and *kevurah* should be piously performed wherever feasible.

BIBLIOGRAPHY

B. Baba Batra 154b
B. Ketubot 11b f
B. Yoma 83a, 84b
B. Sanhedrin 47a
P. Sanhedrin 3 :3
She'eilot u-Teshuvot Noda B'Yehuda Tinyana Yoreh De'ah, no. 210
She'eilot u-Teshuvot Hatam Sofer Yoreh De'ah, no. 336
She'eilot u-Teshuvot B'nei Zion Yoreh De'ah, no. 170
She'eilot u-Teshuvot Maharam Shick Yoreh De'ah, no. 347
She'eilot u-Teshuvot Minhat Eliezer, part 4, no. 24
She'eilot u-Teshuvot Melamed L'Ho'il, part 2, no. 108
She'eilot u-Teshuvot Mishpetei Uziel, part 1, Yoreh De'ah, no. 28
She'eilot u-Teshuvot Malkie Bakodesh, part 3, no. 152
She'eilot u-Teshuvot Or ha-Meir, Rabbi J. M. Shapiro, no. 24
She'eilot u-Teshuvot Sefer Hama'or, Rabbi Eliezer Meir Prail, no. 37–41
She'eilot u-Teshuvot Havalim Banimim, part 3, no. 64
She'eilot u-Teshuvot Atzei Zeitim, Yoreh De'ah, no. 60
Yagdil Torah, 8th year, p. 57, 87, Year 1, p. 112, 3
Rabbinical Council of America Proceedings, 1948, p. 50
Hirsh L. Gordon, "Autopsies according to Jewish Religious Law," *The Hebrew Physician*, v. 1. (1937)
Universal Jewish Encyclopedia under, Autopsy
Dr. Aaron Kottler, "Jewish Attitude to Autopsy", *N. Y. State Journal of Medicine* (May 1, 1957)

6. KASHRUT (1970)

QUESTION: *Is cheese kosher?*

ANSWER: It was May 1945, and I was in Amsterdam, Holland. The German army was still in the city, but officially it had already capitulated to the British who had moved in only a few days earlier. I have reason to believe that Pvt. Irwin Lager, my assistant, and I were the first American soldiers to enter Amsterdam. I came there, not on official orders, but in this fashion. I delivered a Jewish girl who was in hiding in a French monastery during the war to her family that was in hiding in the Dutch village of Vaasen. The village was one hour's ride by jeep from Amsterdam and I could not resist the temptation to go there.

In Amsterdam there were rumors among the surviving Jews who crowded around my jeep that Rabbi Justus Tal, the rabbi of Utrecht who was soon to become the Chief Rabbi of Holland, was also among the survivors. I traced him to the apartment of a Professor van Geldern, professor of Bible at the University of Amsterdam. Our meeting was one of those moments one never forgets. The rabbi was in the advanced stages of starvation and I literally brought him back to life. When I took him out to the street he recited the *Shehecheyanu* for he had not seen sunshine for at least three years. My jeep still had some food supplies left and I wanted to share it with Rabbi Tal. In the supply I had a number of packages of cheese. Rabbi Tal was delighted because he was told that cheese was good for those suffering from starvation. He paused, however, and asked whether the cheese had the proper *hechsher*. When I asked him whether it was proper to ask such questions at a moment like this, he replied, "In my opinion all cheeses are kosher. Since, however, my colleagues disagree with me I have to follow their opinion. The Good Lord did not save me to start breaking the law now." I marvelled at this kind of piety and felt very humble in its presence. Fortunately this cheese was sent to me by my wife and had on it the *hechsher* of Rabbi Joseph Breuer, of the famous Frankfurt-am-Main Breuers, which proved satisfactory even to Rabbi Tal.

Since then, the *kashrut* of hard cheeses had been on my mind. On the one hand, there was the prevalent practice among the observant that hard cheeses were forbidden unless they had a *hechsher;* on the other hand, there were persistent reports that one of the leading luminaries of the Orthodox rabbinate permitted the use of all cheeses but would not allow his opinion to be published. One of the well-known American-trained rabbis was in my house and told me that he, too, followed the same practice. This was strange to me since the very same rabbi had his name on a *hechsher* of a certain cheese. When I asked him why such a *hechsher* was necessary if all cheeses were kosher, he answered that this was to satisfy the *machmirim*—quite a different answer than that of Rabbi Tal.

Since both the *machmirim* and the *meikilim* are honorable gentlemen, we will have to explain the question and see which decision we should follow without violating the law and our conscience.

The talmudic sources for the rules about the permissibility of using of cheeses are the following passages:

> And Bythinian cheeses of the heathen are forbidden, the prohibition extending to any benefit. This is the opinion of R. Meir. But the sages say that the prohibition does not extend to any benefit (B. Avodah Zarah 39b).
>
> R. Judah said: "R. Ismael put this question to R. Joshua as they were on a journey. 'Why,' asked he, 'have they forbidden the cheese of heathens?' He retorted, 'But is not the rennet of a burnt offering more strictly forbidden than the rennet of a carcass?' And yet it was said that a priest who is not fastidious may suck it out raw. Though this opinion was not approved, it was said that no benefit may be derived from it although no trespass would apply thereto. The reason then, R. Joshua said, 'is because they curdle it with the rennet from calves sacrificed to idols.' 'If that be so,' said he, 'why do they not extend the prohibition to any benefit derived from it?' He, however, diverted him to another matter" (ibid).

Another passage to the same effect is:

> The milk in the stomach of an animal of a heathen or in the stomach of a carcass is forbidden. If a man curdled milk with the skin of the stomach of an animal that was validly slaughtered and it imparted its flavor to the milk, it is forbidden (B. Hulin 116a f; Mishnah Hulin 8:5).

The Talmud concludes:

> The law is: One may not curdle milk with the skin of the
> stomach of a carcass, and also with the milk in the stomach
> of an animal slaughtered unto idolatry. One may also curdle
> milk with the milk found in the stomach of a validly slaugh-
> tered animal which had sucked from a *terefa* animal, and
> certainly with the milk found in the stomach of a *terefa*
> animal which had sucked from a valid animal, because the milk
> collected within is considered as dung (B. Hulin 116b).

Note the distinction between *keiva* ("stomach") and *or ha-keiva*
("skin of the stomach"). The term *keiva* refers to the contents of
the fourth stomach, i.e., the milk in the stomach of a suckling calf
in its various forms, liquid or coagulated. There is a difference of
opinion regarding the status of these contents. Alfasi, Maimonides,
and Karo maintain that these contents are not considered as milk.
Rashi is of the opinion that these have the status of milk. Rabbenu
Tam compromises maintaining that if the milk has already jelled,
it loses the status of milk; if it is still in a liquid state, it has the
status of milk. The Ramo follows the opinion of Rabbenu Tam.
(*Arukh ha-Shulhan Yoreh De'ah* 87:34) *Or ha-keiva* refers to the
wall of the stomach of a young calf. Even the ancients knew that
the walls of the stomach curdled milk and therefore used them in
cheesemaking. While the Talmud permits the use of the milk found
in the stomach of a calf for the making of cheese, it forbids the use
of the walls of the stomach for such purposes (B. Hulin 116b).

On this basis, all the *posekim* have forbidden eating cheeses made
by Gentiles. While the Talmud gives a number of reasons for this
issur, Maimonides gives only the one which forbids eating cheeses
of Gentiles because of the suspicion that they use the wall of the
calf's stomach as a curdling agent. Maimonides goes further and
forbids all cheeses of Gentiles, even if it was known that they used
a vegetable as a curdling agent, on the ground of *lo pelug*, that we
do not make any distinctions in a case like this. (Mishneh Torah
Laws Concerning Forbidden Foods 4:13, 14, 19). This opinion is
folowed by the *Tur Yoreh De'ah* 115; the *Levush* (87:10; 115:2)
and Karo (*Yoreh De'ah* 115:2)

Since the curdling agents used in the making of our cheeses is
rennet that is extracted from the walls of the calf's stomach, we
have here a very clear decision that such cheeses may not be eaten.

And yet we discover some dissenting voices even among the early authorities (Rishonim). Rabbenu Tam, for example, says:

As of now we have not found a clear and simple reason for forbidding the cheeses of the heathen since the reason for forbidding these was the fear that a snake may have bitten into them as given by R. Joshua ben Levi, and we have accepted the principle that the law is decided according to the opinion of R. Joshua ben Levi even when his opinion is in disagreement with R. Johanan, how much the more so when it is Samuel. Rabbenu Hananel concurred with this. In the Seder Tanaim v'Amora-im, the law is decided according to the opinion of R. Joshua ben Levi everywhere. . . . Nor is there the apprehension that they may have mixed in the milk of an unclean animal as we have explained above according to the comment of Rashi, for the heathen will not be that foolish to mix in the milk of an unclean animal since such milk does not curdle. Therefore the reason must be the apprehension that a snake may have bitten into it. Since there are no snakes in our area, however, there is no reason for such apprehension. Nor is there reason to object on the ground that the matter was decided upon by vote and another vote is required to reverse the decision, because obviously when they forbade it in the first place it was only in localities where snakes are about. . . . Furthermore, in many places these cheeses are eaten because flowers are used as the curdling agent. Also, the Masters of Narbonne allowed these cheeses in their areas on the ground that flowers were used as the curdling agent. In places where the stomach is used as the curdling agent, however, Rabbi I. ben Chayim said that there was somewhat of a reason to forbid it because they salt the contents of the stomach in its skin and this would make it forbidden on the ground that it constitutes the mixing of milk and meat, inasmuch as salting puts the material in the category of hot food." (B. Avodah Zarah 35a, s. v., *Hada K'tana*).

And now to jump almost a thousand years to a most recent of the later authorities (Aharonim) who says:

Those skins of the stomach or other intestines that are dried until they become like wood, and then filled with milk, are permissible inasmuch as they become so dry that they are like mere wood and do not have at all any of the juices of meat in them. Nevertheless, one should not do so from the start (*lekhat'hilah*). It appears to me that the same applies to curdling cheese with it, that it is forbidden to do so from the start; but if it has been done already it is permissible (*Hakhmat Adam* 40:9).

This is based on the Ramo who says:

The stomach skin is sometimes salted, then dried and it becomes like wood; then they fill it with milk. This is permitted inasmuch as it has become dry it became like a mere piece of wood and there is not any meat juice in it (*Yoreh De'ah* 87:10).

To this the Shach adds:

"Anything that has become dry at the beginning and which became like a piece of wood so that it has no sap in it, even though later it became juicy and damp, it does not affect it" (*Yoreh Deah* 114, subsection 21, quoted in *Darkei Teshuvah* 87:133).

To this the *Arukh ha-Shulhan* adds:

In our place they make cheeses by means of the skin of the stomach that has been dried until it became a powder, together with some other things, as is well known (*Aruch ha-Shulhan, Yoreh De'ah* 87:43).

There are a number of recent responsa that have taken these opinions into consideration and permitted certain cheeses that surely would have been forbidden by the talmudic ruling against the cheeses of the Gentiles. The matter, therefore, needs further clarification.

Cheese and Cheesemaking

First we have to become acquainted with the composition of cheese, the ingredients used, and the process by which it is made. To an uninitiate like myself, it was surprising to learn that the ingredients of the several hundred types of cheeses that are available on the market and the process of making them are very similar. The ingredients are: Milk, a starter, and a coagulant or a curdling agent. The milk is poured into a large vat. To this is added a starter consisting of lactic acid bacteria that sours the milk (i.e., changes its lactose into lactic acid). Then a coagulant is added which curdles the milk. The whey, the liquid left after the solids have curdled, is drawn off. The curd is worked over according to the kind of cheese being made. Finally the cheese is stored to ripen. Ripening is accomplished by various bacteria, molds, or both.

Variations in this process, in the milk used, whether it is cow's milk, or sheep's or goat's, the amount of coagulant, the temperature, the length of the aging and ripening, account for the large array of cheeses known to the world.

The question now is wherein does the *issur* lie? To those people who shun *halab akum* or rather insist on *halab Yisroel*, the answer is obvious. The milk supplied by Gentile farmers without the presence of one of *aheinu b'nei Yisroel* is itself a source for the *issur*. The reason for it is that the milk may be adulterated; the Gentile farmer may have added to it the milk of a forbidden animal (*Yoreh De'ah* 115.1). But this apprehension does not apply to cheese, since it was believed that the milk of nonkosher animals does not curdle (ibid. 2). I have not been able to ascertain the reason that the authorities had this impression. We know that there are cheeses made from camel's and mare's milk. (See Frank Kasikowski, *Cheese and Fermented Milk Foods*, p. 2, 32.)

Then there is the fear that the curdling agent used comes from a forbidden source. The curdling agent is rennet which may come from a plant, from the stomach of a calf that has been validly slaughtered, or from one that is either *neveilah* or *terefah*. When the curdling agent comes from a plant, the rennet is obviously kosher; if it comes from the stomach of a calf that has been validly slaughtered, the rennet is kosher—but we have the problem of *basar be-halab* ("mixing meat and milk"), and the cheese should therefore be forbidden. To this the *posekim* answer that the amount of the coagulant is so infinitesimal that it is *batel beshishim*. The principle of *davar hama'amid afilu b'elef lo batel* ("a coagulant is not neutralized even by a thousand times its bulk") does not apply here since it is not *davar ha-assur* and becomes forbidden only when in contact with another substance, i.e. milk (Maimonides, Mishneh Torah, Laws Concerning Forbidden Foods, 9:16), We still have the problem of *ein mevatlin issur lekhat'hilah* ("one may not proceed deliberately to neutralize a forbidden thing"). To this we answer that the principle applies only when one takes a food article that is forbidden to eat and mixes it with food that is permitted, and the volume of the permitted food is sixty times that of the forbidden food in order to make the forbidden food edible too. Where the article is added as a coagulant or a catalytic agent or as a coloring agent the principle does not apply (*Darkhei Teshuvah* 99:35; *Yad Malakhi, Kelalei Dinim, os aleph*, sec. 260).

This leaves the rennet taken from the wall of the stomach of a calf that is *terefa* or *neveila*. Here the principle of *davar hama'amid afilu b'elef lo batel* ("a coagulant is not neutralized even by a thousand times its bulk") does apply and, hence, even though a very small amount is used, the cheese is forbidden. Maimonides, however, forbids all cheeses, even those in the production of which a vegetable coagulant was used.

My suspicion is that the *issur* in the Talmud is of a different category than that which obtains today. It is linked with the practice of idol worship and the constant suspicion that the foods of the Gentiles are mixed with forbidden ingredients. I sensed that today we have to operate within another frame of reference. To clarify the situation I followed the advice of the Book of Proverbs, paraphrased with apologies to Sholom Aleichem. *Leikh el nemalah atzel* —"go to the cheesemaker you wise man." *Re'eh derakheha*—"see how cheese is made and you will know what you are talking about." I went to a small cheesemaking establishment near Buffalo to see for myself. Though it was a one-man affair, I learned a great deal. The owner had a large vat that would hold hundreds of gallons of milk. He would pour in the milk and the other necessary ingredients by himself. I asked him what induced him to go into the cheesemaking business. He replied that his father came to America from Switzerland; since he was not a watchmaker, he evidently had to be a cheesemaker. He brought with him a supply of dried calf stomachs and that put him into the cheese-producing business. The skins lasted him for a very long time because all he did was snip off a small piece of the dried up stomach and throw it into a large container of milk and the milk would curdle.

I also learned that cheesemaking as a large-scale industry, was comparatively new. It used to be a cottage industry, i.e., each farmer used his milk for drinking, for making butter, and for making cheese. Having grown up myself in a village in the Carpathian

Mountains, I remember my own mother churning butter and curding cheese. It was all done at home, hence the *hashashot* of the rabbis about mixing in other ingredients or smearing the surface of the cheese with lard. This type of cheesemaking is disappearing and is certainly not a factor in the cheeses we buy in the market.

I asked the owner where I could observe cheesemaking on a large scale. I also wanted to know where I could observe the manufacture of rennet. He showed me the rennet he was using. It was not the dried-up stomach skin used by his father, but a liquid that came in large bottles and was manufactured in Milwaukee. He also told me that the great cheese factories were in Wisconsin where more than half the cheese manufactured in the United States comes from. I contacted rabbis in Milwaukee and in Madison to arrange for appointments in their cities. Rabbi Victor Zwelling was particularly helpful in making contacts for me and taking me to these places.

These visits reminded me of the experiences of the Hatam Sofer. His famous responsum on the kashering of glazed or lined or enameled dishes for Passover involved a visit to a factory to discover what material the lining was made of. His decision was to forbid, not because he found out the nature of the material and classified it as *keli heres* ("earthenware"), but rather because the owner of the factory accused him of being a spy for his competitor and showed him the door.

At first my hosts considered me a tourist whose sightseeing program included a visit to a cheese factory. When my questions began to be a bit pointed and not the usual questions a tourist asks, they became cautious, told me that I wanted to know too much, and by rights they should not give me the information that I sought. I had to assure them that I may have been a tourist of a different kind, but I definitely was not in the employ of any competing firm. Even then it was not easy sailing. However, I did obtain the information I wanted.

It was by sheer coincidence that though my visit in both cases, was just to see how these products are manufactured, I chanced upon factories that supplied the kosher trade. I was thus able to see the differences between the kosher and nonkosher products.

In the cheese factory where the kosher cheese was made, the main product was not kosher cheese. It was an ordinary cheese factory, but on certain days a *mashgiach* came down from Chicago and supervised one of the sections where the kosher cheese was made. I was told that he brought his own rennet with him. Whether this was a vegetable compound or it came from the stomach of a kosher slaughtered calf, or a rennet which had a *hechsher* though it came from a nonkosher animal, I was not able to ascertain since the *mashgiach* was not there on the day I visited the factory. I did discover, however, that all the other ingredients were the same as of the other cheeses. Only the rennet had to come from a kosher source.

We therefore should ascertain the status of the rennet, how it is manufactured, and the difference between kosher and nonkosher rennet.

Let me repeat that since the manufacture of cheese has become an industry subject to government regulation, all the *hashashot* of adulteration with nonkosher ingredients fall by the wayside. The Pure Food and Drug Law has been a far more efficient *mashgiach* than all the rabbinic supervisors. Generally, the label on the product is the most reliable guide to the ingredients used, and the government's sanctions for violation are a greater deterrent than the threat of a withdrawal of rabbinic endorsement.

The rennet factory that I visited in Milwaukee produces rennet for both the kosher and nonkosher trade. The label on the finished product enumerates the following ingredients: extract of rennet, salt brine, propylene glycol, sodium benzoate, flavor and color added.

The kosher rennet omits one ingredient—propylene glycol— ostensibly because it has glycerine in it. In all other respects it is the same as the nonkosher product. Parenthetically, the amount of propylene glycol is 0.1%. Since it is not *davar hama-amid*, it certainly is *batel beshishim*. Furthermore, since it is an end-product of a number of chemical changes, there is good reason to maintain that the product should not be considered forbidden. (See *Archives of the Rabbinical Assembly* L88) The Rav Hamchshir is a most prominent member of the Agudat ha-Rabbanim.

It will be best then that we start again from the beginning. What is rennet and how is it produced? The Oxford Dictionary defines rennet as curdled milk found in the stomach of an unweaned calf, or preparation of stomach membrane or of kinds of plants, used in curdling milk for cheese.

For our purpose we have to narrow the definition to include only "the preparation of stomach membrane of unweaned calf." To use the terms of the trade: "Rennet is the enzymatic extract from the fourth stomach of a butchered young calf." (*Cheese and Fermented Milk Foods,* Frank Kosikowski, p. 218)

This enzyme is extracted either from the fresh or from the dried fourth stomach of the calf. Either fresh or dried strips of mucosa cut from the stomach are used. There are three principle methods used for the preparation of rennin or rennet by extraction from fresh or dried fourth stomach of young calves: the Blumenthal process, the hydrochloric process, and the Keil process. (*The Chemistry and Technology of Food and Food Products,* Jacobs, M.B. ed. Interscience Publishers, Inc., New York, 1951, pp. 2352–2354) Each one of these processes sound very complicated to the layman; we know enough, however, to realize that while only in the Blumenthal process is the calf stomach dried before processing, in all cases the process involves a number of chemical changes, and in each case much hydrochloric acid is used.

In the case of the rennet extracted by the Blumenthal process, where the stomach is thoroughly dried, we have the authority of the Ramo, quoted above, to the effect that since the skin of the stomach was dried, it is considered as a mere piece of wood, i.e., it ceases to be a food (*Yoreh De'ah* 87:10).

Where the stomach is not dried the mucosa goes through chemical changes and is subjected to treatment by strong acids. In such cases we have the authority of R. Chayim Ozer Grodzinsky that the product is considered a *davar hadash* and therefore permitted. Let us quote the relevant passage:

> So also it seems to rule in the case of chemical actions that break down a compound and extract from it another substance, as the juice of the stomach called pepsin. And although it certainly would appear that in a substance forbidden by the Torah, all that is latent in it also forbidden and is considered part of it, nevertheless, since it is impossible to extract this latent substance except by drying the forbidden substance and causing its taste to deteriorate, we consider it as a substance, a food the taste of which has been marred (*notein ta'am lefgam*). Even if it is possible to improve the flavor by chemical means the situation remains because it is like a new substance that has come into being (*Responsa of R. Chayim Ozer Grod-*

zinsky, Achi-ezer, part 4, chapter 11; See also, *Enzymes and Food Processing*, Gerald Reed, Academic Press, N. Y., 1966, p. 136, 276).

This is not all, however. Today the rennet is not applied in its pure form. The commercial product that is put on the market is not pure rennet. Following is a description of the process and a detailed account of the ingredients and their amounts used in the manufacture of rennet.

CHEESE AND FERMENTED MILK FOODS

Cornell Commercial Coagulator
(For 10-Gallon Lots)

Procedure

Ingredients

(All technical food grade)

16 grams citric acid
145 grams sodium phosphate Na H_2PO_4
4,000 grams sodium chloride NaCl
900 grams propylene glycol
3,000 grams dark brown sugar

1. Place the above ingredients in a clean 10-gallon milk can.
2. Fill the can, about ¾ full, with clean water and stir the ingredients until a solution is formed.
3. Add 1,000 ml. (cc.) of fresh, single-strength rennet extract and stir.
4. Add enough additional water to fill the 10-gallon can. The final pH should be 4.0 ± .2.
5. Check for optimum activity of the coagulator by filling a Marschall rennet cup with fresh, raw milk at 90°F (32.2°C). As the departing milk drops to the first top line, quickly add 15 ml. of Cornell coagulator solution to the cup and stir.
6. A clot should form in the cup approximately ¾ of the way down. On a Marschall cup of lines numbered 1 to 10, the optimum activity is attained when the curd formed in the cup rests between 6 and 7, and for a cup of lines numbered 1 to 5, it is attained when the curd forms between 3 and 4.

Filling Containers

The color should be clear amber without visible particles. Fill clean, brown, gallon jugs with the mixture; cap and store in a cold place for up to six months.

Cottage cheese is usually set with 26 ml. Cornell commercial co-agulator per 1,000 pounds of skim milk.

Purposes of Ingredients

Citric acid and sodium phosphates form buffers to adjust and maintain the pH of the mixture at 4.0 where rennin is most stable.

Sodium chloride maintains the high activity of the rennin. Propylene glycol preserves the solution against mold, yeast and bacteria.

Brown sugar is used for psychological reasons and as a preservative.

An amber color in the sugar convinces cheesemakers of the authenticity of the coagulator.

Rennet extract is the source of the enzyme, rennin, for the curd formation of milk.

(*Cheese and Fermented Milk Foods*, Frank Kosikowski, p. 90)

You could even say that the rennet is *batel beshishim* within the other materials used. In this case you cannot object on the ground of the principle *davar hama-amid afilu be-elet lo batel* because it is not a *davar hama-amid* in relation to the other ingredients as it is to milk.

Now we have to explain why so many of the *posekim* have forbidden such cheeses. They certainly are not in the category of *katley kanya*. To this I humbly submit the answer that first of all there is a general reluctance to permit anything that was once forbidden, even if the reason for forbidding it does not exist any longer. We mentioned before the principle of:

> "A matter that was forbidden by vote requires another vote to permit it again." And since there is no central body to take such a vote they see no change possible.

There is also the general feeling *kol hayotzei min ha-issur assur*, that once a substance has the status of *issur*, it and anything coming out of it remain so forever. The idea that, sometimes, the substance and what is derived from it cease to be a food, and hence, are in a new and different category is hard to accept though there is ample precedent for it in the Talmud. In the Talmud things are permitted because they are *pirshe be'alma* ("mere dung") or *nifsal m'achilat kelev* ("it became unfit even for the consumption of a dog"), and because *kal hansrafin afran mutar,* ("The ashes of burnt sacrifices are permitted"). Another reason is the tendency to retain the status quo as long as there are substitutes about which there is no question. Thus some *posekim* say, why use rennet derived from an animal when it is possible to use a synthetic one.

For that reason even the *posekim* who believed that there was good reason to permit these cheese restricted this permission to *bede-avad* (post facto) but not to *lekhathilah*. (See *Hakhmat Adam* 40:9; *Darkhei Teshuvah* 87; 130; *Shearim Hamtsuyanim b'Halakhah* 35:10) Slowly, however, responsa appeared that permitted the use of these cheeses even *lekhathilah*. The most explicit statement to that effect is the *Arukh ha-Shulhan*, which says:

> Among us they make cheeses by means of the membrane of the stomach that has been dried until it has become a powder, mixed with some other things as is generally known (*Arukh ha-Shulhan Yoreh De'ah,* 87:42).

On this basis Rabbi Hankin gave the following decision:

> Rennet is a fine powder from the lining of the stomach which has been dried out to the extent that it became unfit even for canine consumption. It is ground and mixed with powder and salt. This powder is then used for curdling cheese and for other purposes. In this case the *Arukh ha-Shulhan* has already declared that it is permitted (Rabbi Hankin in *Hapardes,* Iyyar 5722, p. 9; and in *Eidut l'Yisroel,* pp. 173–177).

Rabbi Pesah Zevi Frank was asked the question that concerned rennet blended with another coagulant, and he permitted the cheese on the ground that *zeh vaseh gorem mutar* ("when the end result is caused by two causes—one permitted and the other forbidden—the product is permitted"). (*Responsa Har Zevi,* sec. 82.)

Rabbi Unterman, the chief rabbi of Israel, was asked a similar question. It concerned rennet imported from Denmark with a *hechsher* of Rabbi Melchior. Rabbi Melchior based his *hechsher* on a *teshuvah* of Rabbi Zirlson of Bucharest. Rabbi Unterman sanctioned its use on the grounds of the principle *zeh vazeh gorem mutar,* inasmuch as there were other ingredients. He also brings in the factor of chemical transformation. Cautiously he adds that although he himself would not consider chemical transformation as adequate reason to make a forbidden substance permissible, he admits it as a consideration in combination with other factors that would make it permissible. (*Or Hamizrah,* Teiveis 5717, p. 9)

The most elaborate explanation for permitting the use of rennet for cheese is found in *Sheilot u-Teshuvot Havalim Banimim* of Rabbi Yehudah Leib Graubart. The editor of the halakhic journal, *Hapardes,* asked him to give his opinion on whether rennet could be used in the making of cheese and in the making of a product called junket. His answer is that it may be used on the following grounds:

a. Since the skin of the stomach, whence it comes is thoroughly dried it ceases to be a food and becomes permissible for use.
b. The rennet is not used by itself, but always in conjunction with other substances.
c. The rennet is produced by a process that involves many chemical changes and it is therefore a *davar hadash.*

The author then marshals all the strictures against this thesis and deftly, and with great scholarly acumen, answers them. And, of course, for each of his assertions, the author brings ample support from authoritative sources.

Thus, for example, the stricture that *davar hamamid afilu be'elef lo batel,* he answers that the principle applies only in the case of an edible food, but not where the coagulant has ceased to be a food.

To sum up: It is our considered opinion that commercial cheeses, all of them, including those in which rennet from any animal, kosher or nonkosher is used as the curdling agent, should be permitted.

We want to add the following considerations. Those of *aheinu benei Yisroel* who are *mahmirim* and are *makpidim* on *halav Yisroel* will naturally not accept our conclusion. Those of the rabbinic authorities who do not accept the principle of *davar hadash* will not accept our *heter* either. Nor will those who do not accept the Pure Food and Drug Law as a protection against adulteration. All these have a right to their opinion and consider themselves blessed on the principle *kol hamahmir tavo alav berakha.* As for us, we say: *Ano lo hilek yadana v'lo bilok yadana, ano shmata yodana.* We cannot be *yotsim l'khal hadei'ot* and pay attention to every dissenting opinion when there is good solid ground upon which to base our opinion.

The rennet used today cannot be considered forbidden because, first, most of it is derived from dried up skins that are *eitz be'alma* ("mere wood"). In addition, the extraction is effected by the use of strong chemicals and acids which removes the substance from the status of a food (*nifsal me-akhilat kelev*). And third, the rennet goes through a number of chemical changes that transform it into a *davar hadash*. And finally, the rennet is not put into the milk in a pure form but is diluted with other substances so that it is *batel beshishim*. Hence, we say *yokhlu anavim veyisba'u,* and we have decided that all the usual cheeses on the market, that list the ingredients hard as well as soft, domestic as well as foreign, are kosher, *beli shum hashash.*

BIBLIOGRAPHY

Mishnah Abodah Zara 4:4-5; Hulin 8:5

B. Abodah Zara 39b; Hulin 116b.

Tosafot Abodah Zara 35a, s.v., *Hada K'tana;* Me'iri Abodah Zara, *ad loc.*

Maimonides, Mishneh Torah Laws Concerning Forbidden Foods. 4:13, 14, 19

Tur Yoreh De'ah 115

Bet Yosef, Tur Yoreh De'ah 115, s.v., *gevinot akum*

Yoreh De'ah 115:1, 2; 87:10; Shach 114:21

Levush, Yoreh De'ah 87:10; 115:2

Tiferet Yisroel on Mishnah Aboda Zara 2:5, in Boaz, sec. 2

Arukh ha-Shulhan Yoreh De'ah 87:34, 43, 43

Darkhei Teshuvah 87:133, 134; 99:35

Hakhmat Adam 40:9

She'arim Hamtzuyanim be'Halakha 35:10

She'eilot u-Teshuvot MaHaRiTaTs, no. 81

She'eilot u-Teshuvot Noda B'Yehudah, Orah Hayim, no. 37

She'eilot u-Teshuvot Ahi-Ezer, part 4, no. 11

She'eilot u-Teshuvot Havalim Banimim, Yoreh Deah, no. 23

She'eilot u-Teshuvot Har Zevi, v. 1, no 82

Hapardes, Iyar 5722 p. 9.

Rabbi Hankin, *Edut l'yisroel* pp 173–177

Rabbi Issar Yehudah Unterman, *Or Hamizrah,* Teiveis, 5713, p. 9.

Archives of Rabbinical Assembly Law Committee

Frank Kasikowski, *Cheese and Fermented Milk Foods*

Jacobs, M. B., *The Chemistry and Technology of Food Products*

7. THE KASHRUT OF GELATIN (1969)

QUESTION : *Is gelatin kosher?*

ANSWER : Behind this question is a history of violent controversy and has aroused spirits beyond the confines of the halls of learning and the cloistered studies of rabbis.

In 1952, *Hapardes,* the well-known halakhic journal which is considered as virtually the house organ of the Union of Orthodox Rabbis of America and Canada, devoted many columns in almost every issue of that year to a discussion of the question. The controversy was sparked by a *hechsher* issued by two prominent rabbis, members of the Union of Orthodox Rabbis for a food product that contained gelatin.

Some of the leading lights of the Agudat ha-Rabbanim (Union of Orthodox Rabbis) challenged the *hechsher* and attacked its author as guilty of permitting the consumption of a food product that was patently forbidden, and demanded therefore that the *hechsher* be revoked. Rabbi Eliezer Silver, who led the battle, issued a responsum in which he marshaled a host of authorities in support of his opposition.

As a result of these sharp protests, the *hechsher* to the product was revoked. This did not mean that the authors of the *hechsher* were convinced of their error and yielded to superior learning. I have documentary evidence to the contrary : The authors remained convinced that their *hechsher* was halakhically valid. In revoking it they simply yielded to pressure which, mildly speaking, was quite heavy-handed.

After a few years had passed and the air was cleared, food products containing gelatin and bearing a *hechsher* of members of the Agudat ha-Rabbanim appeared again on the market without any of the former verbal pyrotechnics.

This controversy was reflected also in the proceeding of our law committee. Whereas before the above-mentioned *hechsher* appeared the decision was not to permit any products containing gelatin. In 1952 the question was presented again and yours truly was assigned the task of preparing a responsum on the question. (See *Archives of the Law Committee*, 1936–1937, p. 331; 1951, p. 44; 1952, E125; 1953, H153.)

Due to personal circumstances, my work was interrupted and Rabbi Salamon Faber was requested to pursue the problem. In treating the question, Rabbi Faber sought the advice of the Law Committee on how to define *davar hadash*: Should we follow the traditional empiric definition or the scientific concept of the term? The Law Committee did not reach a decision on the point and Rabbi Faber discontinued his research on the question. In 1961, the chairman of the Law Committee asked me to reconsider the question. Hence, this responsum.

First, we shall try to describe the process of the manufacture of gelatin.

Gelatin is produced from dry bones of animals (kosher and non-kosher) and also from the skins of these animals. The bones are dried usually from a period of six months to a year. At the end of the drying period, the bones become hard and dry as wood. The bones then undergo a long chemical treatment during which they are treated with hydrochloric acid, salt, lime, and other chemical compounds.

The skins used for the manufacture of gelatin are dried until they become hard and brittle. Then they are treated with chemicals such as hydrochloric acid, salt, lime, etc., as in the case of bones. The skins are freed of all moisture, fat, meat, and its appearance and substance are thus completely changed.

After the bones and the skins have undergone the above chemical treatments, they are placed in large vats of running water which removes all the impurities caused by the chemical treatment of the skins and bones. The substance is treated again with chemicals, washed again, then transferred to large extractors where hot water is used to convert the substance into the final product, gelatin.

For a detailed scientific description see; "Gelatin . . . How It Is Made," in *Food Processing*, November 1967, p. 74ff; *This Is Gelatin*, a pamphlet published by Swift & Co.; *Gelatin*, a pamphlet published by the Gelatin Manufacturers Institute of America in 1962.

It is thus evident that gelatin is the end-product of a process in which a substance is treated chemically and transformed into what seems ostensibly to be a new substance. To decide whether this

end-product is kosher, we shall have to answer the following
question:

a. What is the status of bones? When the carcass of an animal is
declared not kosher—of the class of animals declared clean in
the Bible but because of a certain blemish or because it has not
been slain according to the prescribed law has been declared
treif, or an animal that died naturally, or of the class of animals
declared unclean in the Bible—are its bones included in that
declaration? Thus if the bones of the above three categories are
purged of any food particles such as the meat that is attached
to the bones, or the marrow within them, or food substances
absorbed in it, are these bones considered a food and are they
thus included in the *issur* that applies to the carcass, or do they
cease to be a food, become what the Talmud terms a mere
piece of wood, and thus are not included in the *issur*?

b. Should we decide that the bones have the same status as the
rest of the carcass and is included in the *issur,* is it possible to
change that status by subjecting the bones to the chemical treatment which transforms the bones so that they become a new
product and cease to be a food?

c. Should we grant that the *issur* is removed from the bones because of the chemical transformation which made it lose the
status of food, is this status permanent or may this substance
reassume the status of *issur* when by some process it becomes
edible again?

d. When we speak of a product losing its status as food, do we
have objective measures that brook no exceptions or do we take
into consideration subjective feelings, as when the producer
creates this stage when the substance is not a food as a prepara-
tory step to a stage when it is a food?

e. Do we differentiate between the end-product as a food eaten by
itself and as, rather, an ingredient of a food serving another
food as a binder or a coagulant but not edible in itself?

f. If we should establish the principle that a chemical or a natural
transformation creates a *davar hadash* and removes the *issur,*
do we apply this principle to bones only or do we follow it to its
logical conclusion and apply it also to other substances such as
skin and meat?

g. How do we define the term *davar hadash*?

The authorities that treat this problem all refer back to a responsum of the famous Rabbi Chayim Ozer Grodzensky (1863–1940) who was rabbi in Vilna and the recognized halakhic authority of his day. He was asked about "a new product, a powder derived from dry bones which is blended with numerous other foods, and is also used as a binder for a variety of other foods." They took these dry bones, soaked them in acid, then they put the bones in water mixed with other substances, passed the bones through phosphor, boiled them, cleaned them, and dried them. The bones become dry in forty-eight hours. Then they grind them like powdered sugar. *She'eilot u-Teshuvot Ahi'ezer*, v. 3, no. 33.

His answer was that the product was permissible since dry hard bones are surely not considered as forbidden foods.

We shall bring the sources cited in the above responsum and those most commonly quoted by the other authorities that dealt with the question.

The earliest and most explicit statement is:

"And of their flesh we shall not eat" (Leviticus 11:8), but the bones you may (*Torat Kohanim*, Shemini 4:8).

The source most quoted is the following statement in the *Shulhan Arukh* of R. Joseph Karo.

If a nonkosher piece of meat fell into a vessel containing kosher food, when we apply the principle of *batel beshishim*, the bones attached to the nonkosher meat are counted with the kosher food rather than with the forbidden. (*Yoreh De'ah* 99:1) The obvious reason is that the bones are not forbidden.

The talmudic source for the opinion is the following statement in the Jerusalem Talmud. The shells of a forbidden food are counted, not with the forbidden food, but with the permitted when an accidental mixture occurs (P. Orlah 1:7).

From this prescription the Taz concludes: The bones that are part of a forbidden food, inasmuch as they are not edible are not liable to prohibition.

Rabbi Abraham Yehiel Danzig (1748–1820), a much later authority, in his popular and widely accepted code *Hokhmat Adam* says this much more explicitly.

Whatever the Torah has forbidden [to eat] applies only to substances that are edible, as it is written: Ye shall not eat any carrion. It is so with all forbidden substances. Therefore, bones whether of carrion or of animals that have become *treifa* or of any other forbidden things that are hard [i.e., inedible] that have not in them any fluid [sap or juice] are permitted because they are mere bones. (*Hohmath Adam* 52:1).

The author elaborates this point further and makes a distinction between soft bones and hard bones. Soft bones are counted as meat and only hard bones are included in this permission. He further maintains that although R. Isserles (Ramoh) disagrees with R. Karo in this law, and we usually follow Isserles, in this case Karo is right and we follow his ruling when an appreciable financial loss is involved (*hefsed merubah*). According to these sources bones are not included in the *issur* of forbidden foods because they are not a food.

Obviously this opinion is far from unanimous: According to many authorities bones of forbidden foods are included in the *issur* of these foods. This is clear from the following statement of Maimonides:

> He who eats of carrion, or of *terefah* or of unclean cattle or beasts, or of the hide or of the bones, or of the sinews, or of the horns, or of the hoofs, or of the talons of fowls, at the place when if cut blood will spurt, or of their placenta, even though such eating is forbidden, the act does not entail a penalty because these substances are not edible, and when eaten with meat so that together they are the size of an olive [the size necessary to constitute a transgression of the law that forbids their consumption] they do not count (*Mishneh Torah Laws Concerning Forbidden Foods* 4:18).

In the explicit statement in Torat Kohanim that excludes bones from the *issur* implied in the verse, "And from their flesh ye shall not eat," the exclusion is interpreted to refer to the penalty of lashes (*malkos*) which is entailed by the transgression of a negative commandment.

As to the statement of Joseph Karo that when the bones of non-kosher meat accidentally drop into a pot of kosher meat they are counted with the kosher meat when we apply the principle of *batel beshishim*, these opponents explain it thus: The reason is not that the bones have no *issur* upon them but rather that the bones are devoid of any food with the power of *plitah*. The principle of *batel beshishim* means that the flavor (*ta'am*) of the *issur,* when it has to spread through a volume sixty times its own, loses its identity and has no power to cause another substance to become forbidden. Since the bones do not have their own *ta'am* to spread, they become additional space or volume through which the *issur* has to spread. If, with the bones, there is a volume sixty times the size of the forbidden food, it is a pragmatic fact that it is *batel beshishim.* That, however, does not imply at all that the bones are permitted to be eaten (*Kol Torah,* Nissan 5718, p. 15).

The protagonists who were of the opinion that using bones is permissible, parry these strictures as follows: Maimonides' statement must be construed to refer only to soft bones that are edible and not to hard bones that have been purged of all food content.

The claim that the exclusion of bones from the *issur* implied in the biblical commandment "And of their flesh ye shall not eat" (Leviticus 11:8) refers only to the penalty of lashes is not acceptable. The penalty does not apply in this case for another reason. There is a principle that when forbidden foods used *shelo kederekh akhilatan,* when the eating is not a normal act, there is no penalty of lashes. Eating bones is in that category. Hence, the exclusion must refer to the total *issur* which includes eating. (*Kol Torah,* Sivan 5718, p. 9)

This is not the only source that we depend on. We are told that bones are not in the category of food in another context. The following is an example:

> He who eats of the carrion of fowl that is clean, from the cluster of eggs in it, from the bones, from the sinews, from flesh that has been detached from a living animal, is ritually pure [not contaminated] (B. Beza 7a).

Here it is clear that the bones are not a food and are not in the same category as the flesh of the animal. Of course, there is the ready objection on the principle that *issur mitumah lo yalfinin* (see B. Beza 7a) we do not apply to *issur* principles maintained in the case of *tum'ah.* The *Noda Beyehuda* explains that in this case it is not a derivation (*yalfuta*), but rather a definition (*gilui milta*). We find in the case of *tum'ah* the term *akhilah* does not apply to bones. Therefore, in all cases where the term *akhilah* is used, it does not apply to bones.

It would thus appear that if we should maintain that bones, any bones, are not forbidden, that products that are made or derived from bones are not forbidden. Hence, gelatin made from bones is kosher.

We would like to pursue the matter further and find out whether it is not possible that gelatin made from bones is kosher even according to the opinion that bones are included in the *issur* of the forbidden foods. Since to produce the gelatin the bones have to go through several chemical transformations so that the end product is a *davar hadash*, there is reason to believe that the original *issur* has been eliminated.

On this question too we have an explicit statement by the great halakhic authority, Rabbi Chayim Ozer Grodzensky:

> Likewise it seems to me to decide in the case of chemical actions that break down any compound substance and extract from it another substance, as for instance, juice of the stomach that is called pepsin. Though it would certainly appear that in the case of every substance forbidden in the Torah, all that is latent in it is forbidden, as being part of the forbidden substance; nevertheless, inasmuch as it is impossible to extract the latent substance except by drying the forbidden substance and causing its taste to deteriorate, we judge it as a substance the taste of which has been marred. Although it is possible to improve the taste by chemical means, and by blending it with other substances, it does not change the situation because this is as if a new substance came here and it is therefore like the case of Mosek as interpreted by Rabbenu Nissim, where the substance is deteriorated at the very outset (*She'eilot u-Teshuvot Ahi-Ezer*, part 4, no. 11).

Rabbi Grodzensky refers to *mosek* and the interpretation of Rabbenu Nissim. He also speaks of *panim hadashot ba'u l'kan*, that a new substance has appeared. These deserve elucidation because they both touch upon what is fundamental in this question. The *mosek* is referred to as follows:

> Rav Hisda said in the name of Zeira: For all incense, before smelling them one must pronounce the blessing "who creates spice trees," except in the case of *mosek* which is an animal species, where one pronounces the blessing "who creates species of spices" (B. Berakhot, 43a).

What is this *mosek* that the Talmud calls an animal species? Rabbenu Asher says:

"Some say that *mosek* is the sweat [secretion] of an animal. More proper to say is that a certain animal has a projection [swelling] on its neck. In this swelling a bloodlike substance gathers which subsequently becomes *mosek.*"

Evidently *mosek* is a product extracted from an animal. The dictionary of Ibn Shoshan defines it as follows:

Mosek: 1. an animal of the mammal species, chews the cud, without horns; habitat, the mountains of Central Asia. Its size is that of a hart; the male is distinguished by its upper incisors. They project from the mouth like two long curving dagger blades (moschus). 2. A soft reddish-brown substance with a pungent odor and bitter taste. It is secreted by the male *mosek* by special projections and gathered in a sac near the sex organs. This is used in the manufacture of spices and medical needs. The spice of *mosek* is also mentioned in the Talmud.

Early authorities differ about the permissibility of the use of *mosek*. Rabbenu Asher presents the opinion of Rabbi Zachariah Halevy who maintains that it is forbidden to eat *mosek* because we suspect that it has blood in it. Then he offers the amazing opinion of Rabbenu Yonah who said:

It is possible to give a reason and explain this permission by claiming that the substance is mere waste matter. Though at the beginning it was blood, we take into account its present state. Just as in the case of honey, if a piece of forbidden food fell into it, though the piece melted within the honey [i.e., it was not removed] we consider it as a part of the honey and therefore permissible inasmuch as it is the nature of honey to assimilate to itself substances that fall into it. Here too, though the substance was blood originally, we follow its present state, because it has ceased to be blood; and this is true even if the flavor that it would impart improves the food in which it is used.

That this opinion is amazing is evidenced by the comment with which Rabbenu Asher concludes this opinion: It appears that his supporting evidence itself is in need of support.

Nevertheless, we find here a definite opinion about a condition under which a forbidden food changes its status from a forbidden substance to one permissible, in this case, when the substance that was forbidden because it contained blood has deteriorated so that it is mere waste matter, *pirsha be'alma.*

Before proceeding further we must clarify a number of terms that were used by the quoted authorities. These terms have sometimes been used indiscriminately and therefore caused confusion. We shall try to distinguish between:

1. the term, *nityabesh ha-issur,* refers to a forbidden food that has become dry or rather completely dehydrated and is then compared to *etz b'alma,* a mere piece of wood, i.e., not a food.
2. a substance deteriorates so that it becomes unfit for normal consumption, for which the rabbinic term is *pirsha b'alma.*
3. the term *issur pagum,* that describes a food to which a flavor has been imparted by a proscribed food that spoils rather than improves the whole.
4. the term *panim hadashot,* that refers to a substance that was so processed that it is transformed and changed into something completely new.

Let us explain these and discuss how they affect our question:

1. According to the *Shulhan Arukh,* when a food becomes dehydrated to such a degree that it can be compared to *etz be'alma,* an ordinary piece of wood, it loses its status of a forbidden food. Thus the law is: The skin of the stomach is at times salted and dried and it becomes like wood. It is then filled with milk. This is permissible inasmuch as it was dried until it has become like an ordinary piece of wood and there is no meat fluid in it at all (*Yoreh De'ah* 87:10 in Ramo).

On this the Shach comments: "The same principle applies to the other intestines, if they were dried so they become like wood. Nevertheless, one should not proceed to do so at the start."

This principle is applied not only in the laws of *kashrut.* Thus the *Shulhan Arukh* states:

> There are some who say that in the case of essence of wine that congeals on the walls of a barrel or of jars, the custom is to permit it; because one may use the vessel of Gentiles after a period of twelve months during which it was not used, or after filling and emptying it [with water] and the essence

congealed on it is not peeled off because, inasmuch as it became dry, all the wine moisture in it has gone and it is now
like ordinary dust (*Yoreh De'ah* 123:16).

The same law is applied to blood that has dried completely. Thus
the widely accepted book of responsa, *Shevut Ya'akov*, contains the
following question: "On what did the people rely when they established the usage to permit the drinking of the blood of a ram that
has congealed and dried, a substance called *bucksblut*?" And the
answer, "It appears to me that the reason is that inasmuch as it
has become so dry that it has become like a piece of wood with no
moisture left in it, there is no prohibition against it."

In the case of *hametz* on Passover we also make a distinction
between *hametz nokshah*, *hametz* that has become hard and *hametz*
which has deteriorated to such a degree that it has become unfit
even for the consumption by a dog. Thus we read:

> Leavened bread (*hametz*) that has become mouldy and
> unfit even for a dog's consumption, or if it has been burnt in
> fire before the time for removing *hametz* and it became so
> scorched that it is not fit for a dog, although it is permitted
> to keep it during Passover, it is forbidden to eat it. This is
> true although it cannot be considered a food, but inasmuch as
> one wishes to eat it, it has been raised to that status by his
> intentions and, according to rabbinic enactment, it became a
> food because of his intentions to eat it and is forbidden (*Arukh
> Hashulhan, Orah Hayim*, 442:30).

While this form of *hametz* is not permitted, we see that the drying process has reduced or changed its status. Here, however, we
see a new element that has entered the question, that of thought
and intention. It is possible that a substance which is not edible, is
considered so if a person, by his action, reveals that he considers
it a food. In the subject under consideration this is vital because
the entire process of dehydration is with the intent and purpose of
preparing it to become a food eventually. Furthermore, in modern
food industry, dehydrated foods are very common, and are considered a food even in their dehydrated form because people know
that with some addition of liquid and of other materials these will
become edible.

2. When a substance deteriorates to such a degree that it cannot

be considered any longer in the category of food but rather as
ordinary waste matter (*pirsha be-alma*), it is not forbidden for
consumption. That waste matter even of an animal unfit for food
is permitted according to dietary laws is stated explicitly in the
Talmud. Thus we find: "The ox shall surely be stoned and his flesh
shall not be eaten" (Exodus 21:28); "its flesh is forbidden but its
dung is permitted" (B. Abodah Zarah 34b).

Even more explicit is the following talmudic statement:

> The final decision is that in the making of cheese one may
> not use as a binder the skin [the wall] of the stomach of a
> *nevela* [an animal of the clean species that died without proper
> ritual slaughter], but one may use the stomach [the con-
> tents of it] of a *nevela* or of an animal slaughtered by an idol
> worshipper, and of a kosher animal that sucked from a *terefa*
> animal [the milk in its stomach thus coming from a forbidden
> source], and how much the more so the stomach of an animal
> that sucked from a kosher animal. Why? Because the milk
> gathered in it is ordinary waste matter (B. Hulin 116b fol-
> lowing the version of Tosafot).

On this is based the decision of Maimonides:

> The stomach of a *nevela* and the stomach of an unclean ani-
> mal are permissible because they are like the rest of the waste
> matter in the body. It is therefore permitted to use the stomach
> of an animal slaughtered by an idol worshipper and of an
> unclean cattle or beast, as a binder in the making of cheese
> (Mishneh Torah, Laws Concerning Forbidden Foods, 4:19).

Similarly, the Talmud says:

> Rav Huna said, the skin that comes from opposite the hind
> face of an ass [according to Rashi, it refers to the placenta, the
> afterbirth] is permissible. Why? Because it is ordinary waste
> matter (B. Bekhorot 7b).

Based on this, Maimonides is even more explicit and says:

> The afterbirth of an ass may be eaten because it is like the
> waste matter and urine which are permitted (*Mishneh Torah*,
> Forbidden Foods, 4:20).

Objections are raised that the cases we cited are not similar to
the one under consideration. In the one case, we have the matter of

the substance that always had the status of waste, and we stated that it was never included in the category of forbidden food. In the case of the milk in the stomach, when the concern is that of mixing of meat and milk, the objection is that the milk in itself is not a forbidden food. It is only when it comes in contact with meat that it has the effect of forbidden food, and by that time it had already deteriorated so that it was mere waste matter. (See *Noda be'Yehudah, Yoreh De'ah,* sec. 26) Our question is with food that originally was normal but then has deteriorated to such a degree that it can be considered waste matter. Does it by this process lose its status of forbidden food?

We have good evidence that the *posekim* did not make such a distinction. The Talmud and Maimonides, when they permit the use of the milk in the stomach as a coagulant, include the milk of unclean animals that is in the stomach of either clean or unclean animals. This means that a substance that once had the status of forbidden food (*issur*) now assumes the status of permitted food (*heter*). In the case of *mosek,* that we brought up earlier, one of the reasons that R. Yonah gives for permitting its use is that there is reason to permit it and say that it is ordinary waste matter. This is explicitly the case of an *issur* becoming a *heter*.

On this basis, the *Tiferet Yisroel* permits the consumption of what he calls Wallachian cheese.

> It seems to me that Wallachian cheese, in which a substance called lab, i.e., the milk in the stomach of calves, is used as a binder, may be eaten though the lab was already in the stomach of the calf for days. At all events, the milk itself that is used for the making of the cheese is sixty times as much as the lab. Should you object that a substance used as a binder never loses its identity, we can assume that the lab is congealed and is thus ordinary waste matter (Abodah Zarah 2:5 in Boaz, sub sec. 2).

3. A substance which when mixed with another substance impairs its taste rather than improves it is called *nosein ta'am lifgam.* If the substance having this effect is a forbidden substance, it does not cause the other to become forbidden. The substance which may by itself be edible and good, but when mixed with another food may spoil its taste, and it may be that the substance itself has be-

come putrid and tastes so bad so that it is not fit for human consumption (*Yoreh De'ah* 103, 1–3).

4. The term *davar hadash, panim hadashot,* used by Rabbi Hayim Ozer Grodzinsky reflects an important principle: when a substance goes through a transformation that changes it into something completely new, it also loses its former status in regard to being a forbidden food.

The ancients had no conception of what we, today, call chemical changes. Obviously, they empirically observed objects changing and becoming something else. The most common visible process of such a change is the effect of fire on a substance. The resulting ashes are obviously a new and different substance. Hence they ruled that the ashes of all those things in the Temple which required burning because they could not be used, could be used, since it was a new substance (B. Temurah 34a).

Another form of observable change was when a substance changed its form because it was treated by another substance. The following examples imply or exemplify such a change.

> Rabbi Hanina ben Antigonus said: A kosher animal that sucked from a *terefah* animal is disqualified from being brought upon the altar. (Temurah 5:5) The Talmud explains it as follows:
> What is the reason? Is it because it is fattened by it? In that case if he fed the animal with kernels dedicated to an idol, it should be forbidden. To this Rabbi Hanina Tritaah read before Rabbi Yohanan, it is a case where he made the animal such hot milk every morning so that the animal could subsist on it a whole day [24 hours] (B. Temurah 31a).

The Commentary Bartinoro explains this as follows:

> A kosher animal that sucked from a *terefah* animal is disqualified that day that it sucked, i.e., for twenty-four hours. It is disqualified for a sacrifice because it can subsist on this milk without any other food, and it does not become digested in its intestines until a full day has been completed. After it has become digested in its intestines, however, Rabbi Hanina agrees that the animal is kosher, since everyone agrees that even an animal that has been fattened on vetches dedicated to an idol is fit for the altar.

Thus, when the digestive juices work on a substance they create a *davar hadash*. Another example is this: If an unclean fish swallowed a clean fish [and it was recovered intact] it is permitted to eat it, since it was not bred from the other (B. Bekhorot 7b). As is obvious, this law applies before the process of digestion takes place. After the process of digestion the host assimilates the foreign body, and the foreign substance assumes the status of the host.

Rabbi Moshe Feinstein treats an analogous question. Is the milk and meat of cattle that are fed *hametz* exclusively, even during Passover, permissible for use on Pesah? He maintains that they are permissible, but he makes the following comment: If we could make a machine that would operate like a digestive system, it is inconceivable if the substance was originally forbidden (*issur*) that it should become permitted as a result of the digestive action. He, therefore, makes a distinction between a natural and a mechanical process (*Igrot Moshe, Orah Hayim,* Sec. 147)

We would like to reverse the reasoning. Inasmuch as we accept that a forbidden food that has been consumed and digested by a kosher animal becomes part of the animal and, as such, loses its forbidden status (*issur*) and becomes kosher through the host, if this process were reproduced by a machine, the end product should also be permitted. The distinction between a natural and mechanical process has no halakhic support. (See the above-quoted opinion of Rabbenu Yonah about the nature of honey to assimilate to itself foreign bodies that fall into it.)

It is neither difficult nor incorrect to extend this to chemical changes, which the above-mentioned really were. A substance treated by another substance which transforms it chemically thus becomes a *panim hadashot*. Indeed, Professor David Hoffman says in a similar case:

> And consider "Zametoze" which has come into being by way of chemical processes, has gone through a great change so that a "new substance" has come here. My son Michael (may he live long) who is a doctor, told me that the meat has changed in a way similar to the change taking place in the stomach by means of digestion (*Melamed l'Ho'il,* Vol. 2, responsum 27).

(See opinion of R. Y. Abramsky quoted in *Responsa Tzitz Eliezer,* v. 9, who follows the scientific principle and on that basis claims that it is not a *panim hadashot*. He claims that the substance is abstracted, not transformed. This is not correct scientifically. Halakhically, even if it were correct scientifically, it goes counter to the claim of R. Chayim Ozer, who said:

> Nevertheless, since it is impossible to bring out this potential except through the substance being dried, and its forbidden taste being marred, it is subject to the rules of marred foods (*Responsa Ahi-Ezer*, vol. 3, sec. 33).

We may return to answer the questions we posed at the beginning of our responsum.

The first question we asked was about the status of bones of non-kosher animals, bones that have been purged of all flesh and marrow and dried thoroughly. We have presented sufficient evidence that such bones are not forbidden for consumption. Most of the gelatin used for the manufacturing of Jello is made of such bones. Those most scrupulous can always inquire of the manufacturers whether their product is made from bones. They usually answer such questions gladly. If the gelatin is made of bone it is *kosher limhadrin min hamhadrin*.

However, our main support for a *heter* comes from the fact that in the manufacture of gelatin the materials used go through chemical changes that make the end-product a new product. Both by pragmatic observation and by chemical analysis the end-product is something quite different from the original substance.

There are those who claim, as Dayan Abramsky, does that the collogen from which gelatin is made is not a new substance. All that the chemical treatment does is remove the elements not necessary for the gelatin, such as calcium and other impurities, leaving intact an element that was there all the time and thus not creating a new one. There is no question that there is a chemical change in the collagen itself. (*Food Engineering*, November 1967, p. 75) Even, however, if we should not consider this enough of a change chemically to make it a *davar hadash*, there is enough of a change there from the pragmatic aspect to put it in that category. Furthermore, as Dayan Abramsky says, there are enough other factors in the process to lead us to make it permissible, such as the fact that there is a strong opinion that bones themselves are not forbidden. Furthermore, the opinion of R. Chayim Ozer that when an object is treated with powerful chemicals in order to remove part of it, it becomes permissible because of the principle of *noten ta'am lifgam.* (*Responsa Yoreh De'ah,* sec. 11)

In a recent decision of the Bet Din of London the same principle was applied to gelatin made from skins. (Rabbi Aryeh Leib Grossnass, office of the Bet Din, London) It is when we come to gelatin made from other substances, such as meat and fat, that we meet with the greatest difficulty. There is the persistent insistence on the principle that once a thing has the status of an *issur,* it remains so, no matter what happens.

Psychologically, and logically too, there is a resistance to allowing a *davar issur* to be transformed into a *davar heter.* Now, with the new science of food processing where such a transformation often takes place, a new area of *heterim* will open and as Dayan Abramsky cautions, people will say that it is a matter of caprice with the rabbis whether a thing is permitted or not. I did not need Dayan Abramsky's cautioning. I heard well-meaning lay people say in such cases that the rabbis can twist and turn such decisions to suit their fancy. And yet a sense of responsibility gives us no choice but to follow the halakhic conclusion. Furthermore, the fear for the *hilul hashem* that many *hekhsheirim* entail tempts us to remove as many articles from need of a *hekhsher* as is possible to lessen the area of such *Hilul Hashem, Vedai lehakima.*

To sum up: Gelatin that is made from bone or hides is kosher. Though this opinion is not unanimous there is an increasing number of authorities who consider the product permissible. In the case of gelatin made from the flesh of nonkosher animals there is the strong objection because of the principle of *kol hayotzeh min ha-issur issur.*

To strengthen the case, I would like to add the opinion of the following authorities who maintain that when a substance is completely dry (dehydrated) it loses its status of *davar ha-assur.* The *Shulhan Arukh,* after saying, "a substance as dry as wood is forbidden," adds, some permit even meat that becomes dry as wood, with the additional remark that even if thereafter the substance is cooked or soaked and as a result ceases to be as dry as a piece of wood, it retains its permitted status (*Arukh ha-Shulhan, Yoreh De'ah* 87:43).

The same opinion is voiced in Responsa *Tiferet Zevi,* quoted in *Pit'he Teshuvah, Yoreh De'ah* 87, subsec. 20.

It is therefore recommended that we allow the use of all gelatins.

8. SWORDFISH (1966)

QUESTION : *Is swordfish kosher?*

ANSWER : The Committee on Jewish Law and Standards of the Rabbinical Assembly has ruled in the past that swordfish is kosher. This decision was based on the study of the traditional halakhic sources as well as the evidence of competent scientific experts in the field.

Recently the question has been reopened because of the statement by the Union of Orthodox Congregations based on a statement of Rabbi Moshe Tendler, who is Rosh Yeshiva, Yeshivat Rabenu Yits'hak Elhanan and Associate Professor of Biology, Yeshiva College.

Some of our colleagues have urged that we restudy the question to see whether there is any new evidence that would make us revise our previous decision. Our answer will depend on the resolution of the following two questions : Does the swordfish have scales? Do these scales satisfy the requirements of the Halakhah?

The Bible states :

> These you may eat, of all that live in water : anything in water, whether in the seas or in the streams, that has fins and scales, these you may eat (Leviticus 11:9).
> These you may eat of all that live in water : you may eat anything that has fins and scales (Deuteronomy 14:9).

The Mishnah declares :

> And [the clean] among fishes are all that have fins and scales. Rabbi Judah says any variety that has two scales and one fin. And these are the scales, such as are fixed to the body, and fins, those by whose means it swims (*Hulin* 3:7).

The Gemara comments :

> And whence do we know that the term *kaskasim* means the scales that cover the fish like a garment? Because it is written, "and he was clad with kaskasim [a coat of mail]" (I Samuel 17:5).

> The Rabbis have learned: If it has no scales now but will grow them later, as for example the *sultanit* [spat] and the apian [sardine], it is permitted. If it has scales now, but will shed them later when drawn out of the water, as for example the colias, scomber, swordfish, athrias and tunny, these are permitted.

Based on these sources, Maimonides states:

> Scales are attached to the entire body. If a fish has no scales now, but will have them when it grows up, or if it has scales while in the sea, but sheds them when drawn out of the water, it is permitted (Mishneh Torah, Laws Concerning Forbidden Food 1:24).

The *Shulhan Arukh* follows the same opinion, adding:

> Scales are the "peels" set in it. Says the Ramo: Provided they can be peeled off by hand or with an instrument. If they cannot be peeled off from the skin of the fish they are not called scales (Yoreh De'ah 83:1).

Now the question is whether the swordfish satisfies these requirements.

In the *Talmudic Encyclopedia,* under the article "Dagim," the swordfish is identified as *Xiphias gladius,* a fish which, in its early stages, has scales that disappear when it matures. According to its Latin and Greek names it is suggested that it is the *Akseptias* of the Talmud: Hulin 66b. (*Talmudic Encyclopedia,* vol. V, pp. 207ff).

While there has been some question about this, one of the later authorities whose opinions have been widely accepted says unhesitatingly:

> It is the widespread custom in all Israel to eat the swordfish called "fish ispada" even though it has no scales because it is said that when it comes out of the sea, because of its excitement it shakes and sheds its scales (Darkei Teshuvah 83:16).

Similarly, Rabbi H. P. Tchorch of the Israeli ministry of religion in a report about *kashrut* in Israel discusses the swordfish, and after quoting a number of authorities concludes:

> "From all the above it becomes clear that swordfish is permitted."

Then comes the following:

> "However, a great scientist, and one of the experts in identi-
> fying fish (ichthyologist), Rabbi Moshe Tendler, professor
> at the Yeshiva University in New York, disagrees with the
> manner of classifying this fish. According to him, it becomes
> clear that there are two classes of fish called swordfish [sailfish
> and swordfish]. The first is the "clean" fish, but the second
> is an "unclean" fish. It is then possible to say that the author
> of *Knesset Hagdolah* who permitted the fish ispada, meant the
> latter, which is called "sailfish" (Sinai, v. 32, issues 4–5, p.
> 209).

Evidently this noted scientist and expert ichthyologist has so
overawed his colleagues in the Orthodox rabbinate, that even those
who had permitted it, backtracked. In Israel they concluded that
the matter needs further study.

Since we are neither scientists nor ichthyologists, we turned to
the recognized ones—we have turned to the United States Bureau
of Fisheries—and received an answer from the Ichthyological Laboratory, U.S. National Museum of Washington, D.C.

They sent us copies of letters which had been sent to them earlier
in response to similar questions. In each case, it was stated definitely
and unequivocally that the swordfish has scales in its early stages.
It sheds them when it reaches a certain size. The author of the *issur*
of swordfish nevertheless claims the following:

> The claim that the immature forms do have scales has never
> been confirmed by people in whom we can have confidence.
> Instead, among ichthyologists there is doubt as to "if" and
> "when" they are lost. Since it is difficult to differentiate be-
> tween the young of sailfish and the young of swordfish both
> of whom have similar external characteristics, and only the
> sailfish has scales in the adult form, the halakhic decision
> must preclude the scientific controversy and judge the fish
> as it appears to the observer (November 19, 1964).

Again, not personally being able to sit in judgment on this statement, I turned to Dr. Carl Gans, who holds a PhD degree in zoology,
at the State University of New York at Buffalo. I went to some
lengths to check on the status of Dr. Gans among his peers and I
am satisfied with his reliability as a scientist.

I acquainted him with the problem and had no difficulty conveying it to him since he has a good Jewish background in addition to his scientific competence. His personal opinion was that the swordfish does have scales. When I showed him the letter from the Bureau of Fisheries of the United States Department of the Interior with the signature of Bruce B. Collette, he said that Mr. Collette is a great authority in the field and is most reliable. When I told him that a claim was made that "the claim that immature forms do have scales has never been confirmed by people in whom we can have confidence," he said this certainly cannot apply to Mr. Collette, whom he knows personally. He therefore wrote a letter to Mr. Collette, at my request, to which the following answer came:

> Dear Carl:
> In reply to your letter of December 7 on the swordfish-scale problem, enclosed is a Fishery Leaflet by Isaac Ginsburg on the subject and also a Xerox copy of the Nakamura et al. paper of 1951. As you can see from these references, swordfish do have scales as juveniles. They retain the scales until they are approximately four feet long. This means that most swordfish found in the markets no longer have scales although they once did. Whether this leaves it kosher or not is up to your rabbinical friend.
> > Sincerely,
> > Bruce B. Collette
> > Assistant Laboratory Director

I have, in my personal file, a copy of the studies mentioned in Mr. Collette's letter.* They all conclude that swordfish have scales at some stage of their development. In the government *List of Common Food Fishes that Have Both Fish and Scales*, the swordfish is listed too. On the basis of this evidence, we have to reconfirm our original position that the swordfish is kosher.

Food Fishes with Fins and Scales, by Isaac Ginsburg, Systematic Zoologist, Washington, D.C.: United States Dept. of the Interior, Fish & Wildlife Service, Bureau of commercial Fisheries, Fishery Leaflet 531, December 1961 (7 pages).

"Notes on the Life-History of the Swordfish, *Xiphias gladius Linnaeus*," by H. Nakamura, T. Kaminwa, Y. Yabuta, et al., published in the *Japanese Journal of Ichthyology*, 1951 pp. 264–271, inclusive.

9. GLASS UTENSILS

QUESTION : *Is the use of glass utensils for meat and milk permitted?*

ANSWER : The question of permitting the use of glassware for both milk and meat comes up very frequently before rabbis. The new uses to which glass has been put in the kitchen naturally increases the chances for such questions. Whereas until now glass was used mainly for bottles and for drinking glasses, today they are replacing earthenware and china and even metal pots, if we include Pyrex dishes. Previously, glassware was rarely used for hot foods or liquids ; today, with glass cups, saucers, soup plates, and even frying pans, the question naturally would follow whether we would allow the use of these for both milk and meat. We know that the law is far less stringent with glassware than with any other kind of utensil. Would we go as far as permitting their outright use for all purposes ? The question is an important one, because the decision may make the observance of *kashrut* less expensive and less onerous and we may thereby lessen the rate of defection from the ranks of those who still abide by these laws.

Among the *posekim* there is a difference of opinion that can be traced to the Talmud. On the one hand we read in the Talmud :

> Why did the rabbis impose uncleanness upon glassware? Said R. Johanan in the name of Resh Lakeish, "Since it is manufactured from sand, the rabbis declared it the same as earthernware (B. Kiddushin 78a, Yebamot 60b)."

This puts glassware on a par with earthenware and thus not only forbids its use for both milk and meat, but even makes it ineligible for "kashering." On the other hand, we have another passage in *Abot d' R. Natan* which, though strictly speaking is not included in the Talmud, is quoted by most authorities :

> Three things apply to glass dishes : it neither absorbs nor exudes, etc. (Abot d'Rabbi Natan, chap. 41).

This would make glassware so hard that it cannot absorb and consequently would not need any "kashering" when its use is changed from milk to meat provided the vessels are clean. This cleavage is reflected in the later authorities and is clearly set forth in the last authoritative code, the *Shulhan Arukh*. There, too, we have the difference of opinion between Joseph Karo and Moses Isserles, side by side. Thus, the opinion of Joseph Karo is:

> Glass dishes, even if one puts them into storage, and even if one uses them for hot food, need no kashering since they do not absorb; it is enough to rinse them (Orah Hayyim 451:26).

And immediately following this statement is the comment of Moses Isserles:

> And some are more stringent and say that even purging by boiling (*hag'alah*) is of no effect in their case. And so is the custom in Ashkenaz [Germany] and in these lands (*Orah Hayyim* 451:26).

It is obvious, of course, that though this ruling is applied to the laws of Pesah it applies equally to our question.

Dr. Boaz Cohen has made a study of the sources that mention glassware and has come to the conclusion that opinions are divided geographically, i.e., the Spanish scholars take the more lenient view while the French and the later German *posekim* take the stricter view. I have not been able to study all the sources mentioned and shall quote here those that I could reach and which I believe will be sufficient for our purpose. I have already mentioned Joseph Karo and Moses Isserles. The question is also treated by R. Nissim who says:

> Nevertheless, since the master taught us that there are vessels, that even if put away in storage may be rendered permitted by rinsing because of the paucity of their absorption, it seems simple in my eyes to permit glass dishes by rinsing even if put into storage because they are smooth and hard, and their absorption is less than all other vessels (Ran. Abodah Zarah, chapt. 5. s.v., *v'Yeroka*).

The clearest statement is found in a responsum of Salamon ibn Adret which is most similar to our case because definite mention is made of a specific case where the vessel was used for hot liquids. The responsum is short and we will quote it in full:

And about what you inquired regarding glass dishes that is even used for hot food, whether they need kashering, according to the statement in Abot d'Rabbi Natan. It was taught: glass dishes neither absorb nor exude: the answer is that it is obvious that they need no kashering whatsoever just because they are very smooth, and it thus seems that what is very smooth does not absorb. Furthermore, we see that they do not sweat, i.e., the liquid inside does not seep through, as in the case of earthenware (RASHBA, responsum 233)

The Mordecai cites both opinions without committing himself, from which Dr. Cohen deduces that the practice was not fixed. R. Elijah the Gaon of Vilna in his commentary on the paragraph we quoted from R. Joseph Karo quotes the *Mordekhai* among those who would class glassware with earthenware. We shall quote the opinions mentioned in the *Mordekhai*:

Hence, Rabbi Yehiel of Paris, deduced that those glass tumblers from which they drank the other days of the year, it is forbidden to drink from one of them on Passover even if the hot liquid is poured into them, because they have the status of earthenware inasmuch as they are manufactured from sand. It is so even if they are used for cold food only; nevertheless, since at times they soak crumbs of hot bread in wine, it is like pickling, which is tantamount to cooking.

The RABI Ha-Ezri wrote that glass dishes are smooth and as we said in the case of the heart, do not absorb. Support for this comes from abot d'Rabbi Natan where it says, three things are said regarding earthenware, it absorbs and exudes, keeps what it contains, which is not the case with glassware (*Mordekhai* Abodah Zara, sec. 826).

As far as our practice until now is concerned, being Ashkenazic Jews we followed the ruling of Moses Isserles as the commentators Magen David and Magen Avraham interpret him, i.e., not that glassware cannot be made kosher at all, but rather that in those cases where the glass utensils have already been used with cold liquids only rinsing was necessary, while where it was used with hot liquids *hag'alah* would be necessary. Consequently the code of Rabbi Abraham Danzig contains the following ruling:

Some say that glassware, even if beer is kept in it for many days or months, needs only washing and rinsing, even if it is used for hot food, because glass dishes do not absorb. And there are others who are stringent and say just the opposite, even kashering (*hag'alah*) has no effect on glassware, and this is the custom in these lands. However, if it was done *bede'avad*, we do not apply a strict measure, and therefore, if glassware was used customarily for cold food, it is permitted even without kashering, and if it is used for hot food, or if there is an apprehension that *hametz* stayed in them for over twenty-four hours, kashering has an effect, *bede'avad* (*Hayye Adam*, 125:26).

While the abbreviated code of Rabbi Salamon Ganzfried rules:

It is a custom in these lands that kashering has no effect in the case of glassware (*Kitzur Shulhan Arukh*, 116:13).

With these decisions before us, let us also take into consideration the practical results and aspects of the question. How will the decision affect the attitude of the people? Will it increase the observance of the laws or will it have the opposite effect? For my personal satisfaction I have inquired of several housewives, in such a manner that they could not suspect my ulterior motives, what their attitude would be. Some, of course, would appreciate any amelioration of the laws. Most of them, however, felt that if the ruling would do away with two sets of dishes altogether, it would mean something. To apply the ruling to glassware only would add confusion in the kitchen, especially in those houses where there are maids where it would make it harder for them to explain that of these dishes we have two kinds and of these only one. The plates are the same for both milk and meat, but we must have two kinds of silver. If it is just for glass dishes, they prefer to have the same ruling apply as to the other dishes. From the practical point of view, it would seem to me that to permit the use of one set of dishes with glassware would not improve conditions in *kashrut*. Those who still abide by the laws will continue to do so even if they must have two sets of glass utensils.

Now from the point of view of the law, it seems to me that in all those cases where the lenient attitude was taken, the intimation is that it applies only "*bede'ovad*," but not to "*l'hathiloh*." All the rulings we have quoted are mentioned, not in connection with milk and meat, but in connection with Passover and *yayin nesekh*. In the case of Passover, there is no danger of confusion because the two foods concerned are not usually side by side. When there is *hametz* there are no *Pessahdike* articles, and vice-versa. Thus, whereas theoretically the same ruling would apply to both, from the practical point of view we must differentiate between the two. Then, even there a careful reading of the texts would indicate that we cannot recommend using glassware for milk and meat as a practice since the change must be preceded by at least some kind of cleansing. Where there is a slight danger that the boundaries between milk and meat might be forgotten, it is certainly not advisable to make a practice of using one set of dishes for both.

It is my opinion, therefore, that when an individual question comes up where a milk dish was used for meat or vice-versa, we should follow the lenient attitude of requiring just rinsing, but we should definitely discourage the regular use of one set of dishes for milk and meat.

10. SOAKING FOWL

QUESTION: *Is soaking slaughtered fowl in water heated to 119° F permitted?*

ANSWER: I have been asked whether it is permissible to dip a slaughtered fowl, before salting it, into water that is heated to 119°F so that the feathers could more easily be plucked by a machine.

The source for the law against scalding any meat before salting it is the following:

> Therefore the practice in these countries is not to scald anything [any meats] which has not been salted (*Yoreh De'ah* 68:11).

This would seem to preclude the practice. However, there are certain qualifications and exceptions to the rule. The rule deals with boiling water that is on the fire (*keli rishon*) or with hot water that is poured from such a vessel (*iruy*). There are also opinions that even if the water has been poured from the vessel on the fire into a second vessel it has the same effect (*keli sheini mevashel*). However, in the case of *keli sheini* we make this exception.

> However, in honor of guests or because of Shabbat it is permissible to put frozen meat into a *keli sheini* in order to hasten its salting. It is good to be careful [*Shach:* if possible] to put it into water that does not scald the hand [literally from which the hand shrinks back].

The *Peri Megadim* comments that this is an extra precaution, because for the sake of guests it is permitted to scald fowl even in water that scalds the hand. The *Be'er Heiteiv* adds that if it is not heated so that it scalds the hand it can be done even in *keli rishon*.

In the *Hakhmat Adam* we find this law stated even more explicitly.

> It is forbidden to scald at the start [lekhathilah] a fowl [i.e., to dip it into boiling water in order that the feathers be removed from it] even in a *keli sheini* if it so hot that the hand

84

shrinks back from it because of the heat. If one does it to honor the Sabbath or guests, however, when one needs a large quantity of meat and there is no other way to do it, and the meat is frozen, it is permitted to put into a *keli sheini*, even at the start (lekhathilah). Nevertheless, if it is possible one should put it there only if it does not scald the hand. If it is so hot that the hand gets burned by the water then even a *keli sheini* effects cooking [which is forbidden] (Hakhmat Adm 59:6).

It is evident that if it is *keli sheini* and *ein hayad soledet bo* ("it does not scald the hand") it can be done. The question is: Is 119°F *hayad soledet bo* or not? I asked Dr. Norman Cole, of the Cole Clinic for Small Animals of Buffalo, New York, what happens to a slaughtered fowl that has been dipped into water heated to 119°F. His answer was: "It just gets wet. There is no other internal effect."

Then, in the presence of two other people, I heated water to 119°F and put my hand into it. It was hot, but not what could be called *hayad soledet bo,* because I could keep my hand in it for an extended period of time. To preclude an error in our thermometers, I called Dr. Sheldon Moline at the Linde Chemical Co. of Niagara Falls, New York, and asked him to make the same experiment in the laboratory with tested precision instruments. His reaction was the same. It can become uncomfortable if you keep your hands in it too long. It cannot be called scalding hot.

There are other considerations here that are akin to the exceptions made in the *Yoreh De'ah*—that of Shabbat and guests. We live in an age of automation and mechanization. We should not make it more difficult to observe *kashrut* by preventing mechanization where the Halakhah permits it. The refusal to permit this practice would simply add to the cost of keeping *kashrut* and put another obstacle in the way of the observant and the faithful.

My answer, therefore, is to permit the dipping of slaughtered fowl before salting it into water that is heated to 119°F or less, especially if it is in a *keli sheini*.

11. WARMING FOOD ON SHABBES

QUESTION: *Is it permissible to warm food on the Sabbath?*

ANSWER: The answer to the question depends upon the following factors:

    a. What do we include in the prohibition of *bishul* ("cooking").

    b. Even when not included in *bishul,* an act is sometimes forbidden on the Sabbath because of the apprehension that it may lead to tampering with the fire (*shema yehateh b'gahalim*). Does this apply to the warming of food?

On the first question there is a difference of opinion between Maimonides and the Tur. According to Maimonides we adhere to the principle of *ein bishul ahar bishul* ("once a food is cooked, cooking it again does not constitute cooking"). The Tur, on the other hand, maintains that *yeish bishul ahar bishul* ("food recooked is accounted as cooking"). According to Maimonides it would then be permitted to warm food on the fire even after it was cooled. The decision in the *Orah Hayim* is not in accord with Maimonides.

The present practice is this. Solid food may be warmed under any circumstance. Here we follow the principle of *mitstamek v'ra lo,* solid food when reheated suffers thereby (B. Shabbat 31a). Liquid food may be warmed if not entirely cold. If it is entirely cold, as when it is kept in a refrigerator, it would seem that it is not permitted.

Rabbi Moses Isserles cites an opinion (Maimonides) that it is permitted to warm liquids even when entirely cold, but hastens to add: *V'nahagu lehakel bezeh im lo nitstanen legamri* ("the custom is to be lenient here except in cases where it is cooled completely") (*Orah Hayim* 318:15). However, in the Sha'rei Teshuvah (318:35) it would seem that even liquid food may be warmed if it is done in a manner that will keep it from becoming too hot, as when it is put too near to the fire, which usually causes boiling.

The apprehension of *shema yehateh begahalim* may be overcome by having an asbestos disc or a tin plate on top of the fire, or by not putting the pot directly on the fire. These constitute a *heker*

("a reminder") which will remind one not to tamper with the fire.
To summarize:
Food may be warmed under the following conditions:
a. solid food may be heated under any condition;
b. liquid food when not entirely cold;
c. liquid food when entirely cold but warmed over a fire which
    does not make it too hot;
d. In all these cases the fire must be covered in order to serve as
    a reminder (*heker*) against tampering with the fire.

12. ADVERTISING PRACTICES

QUESTION: *Current business practice condones advertising that borders on misrepresentation but is within the law. What is the attitude of Jewish law to this practice?*

ANSWER: According to the Talmud, when we shall appear before the throne of judgment on high the first question we shall be asked will be: Have you dealt honestly in your business (B. Shabbat 31a). Evidently, the rabbis attached a great deal of importance to ethical conduct in business. A further evidence to that effect is the following declaration: Jerusalem perished only because the people who were honest in business ceased to exist in their midst. (B. Shabbat 149b). This does not mean that the people of Jerusalem were more dishonest than other people. It does mean that the rabbis considered dishonesty in business a sin grave enough to deserve a punishment as severe as the destruction of Jerusalem. The destruction of Jerusalem was a disastrous calamity. It could have come only as a punishment for a most heinous sin. Dishonesty in business is the only crime grievous enough to merit such punishment.

To say that the rabbis were in favor of ethical conduct and against dishonesty in business does not say very much for them. It is like President Coolidge's alleged answer when he was asked what his pastor was preaching about: "Sin." "What did he say?" "He said he was against it." What we should like to do is cite specific current issues that are controversial and explain the attitude of the rabbis toward them.

The items I shall cite are prompted neither by an intrinsic priority nor by a logical sequence nor by intimation on the part of the inquirer, but rather by a book I was reading when preparing the answer, a book that was a best seller for a long time, and hence the items that the question touched on are the subjects treated in the book. I refer to *The Hidden Persuaders*, by Vance Packard. Those who are acquainted with the book know that its theme is the use of psychological techniques in advertising and marketing. Advertisers today search for the secret weaknesses of their customers and exploit them. The last chapter of the book bears the title, "The Question of Morality." Among the questions that the author poses are:

1. What is the morality of manipulating small children even before they reach the age when they are legally responsible?
2. What is the morality of developing in the public an attitude of wastefulness toward national resources by encouraging the "psychological obsolescence" of products already in use?
3. Do we have a right to manipulate human personality?

The rabbis do not answer these questions directly but by implication in many of the legal decisions they have rendered. The first question we mentioned is that of manipulating children. The answer of the rabbis is very clear and unequivocal: "A shopkeeper must not distribute parched corn or nuts to children because he thereby accustoms them to come to him (i.e., when their mothers send them to buy something. This is considered unfair competition). (B. Baba Mesia 60a).

This instance suggests another question, that of packaging. Packaging is, of course, an accepted practice and has become a major industry. When its purpose was the preservation of the article, to make its handling easier, or to facilitate its transportation, no ethical question was involved. When it became, however, the province of the sales department it assumed a new aspect. To illustrate this point we shall cite an instance mentioned in *The Hidden Persuaders*.

> Mr. Cheskin of the Color Research Institute was asked to design two boxes for a candy manufacturer, both two-pounders. One of the boxes was to contain candy to sell for $1.95 to the lower class clientele, and the other box to sell for $3.50 to upper class buyers.
>
> Mr. Cheskin gave the problem his deepest thought and came up with the conclusion that the box for the expensive $3.50 candy could be bought for nine cents, while the box for the cheaper $1.95 candy should have to cost fifty cents.

The reasoning behind this odd conclusion is that the outer package means a lot more to the person giving the $1.95 box, who is not used to buying candy, and the girl receiving the candy will cherish the gift and perhaps save the box if it is nice as a jewelry box.

The person buying the $3.50 candy, on the other hand, gives little thought to the box. It will be thrown away. The candy is what counts.

What do the rabbis of the Talmud have to say about the legitimacy of this practice? Again the rabbis give a very clear answer: "One must not sift pounded beans [to remove the refuse. Because of the better appearance of the beans he advances the price by more than the value of the corresponding weight of the refuse removed, and Abba Shaul forbids it as a fraud]. This is the view of Abba Shaul. The Sages permit it. Yet they admit that he may not pick out the refuse from the top of the bin, because in this case the only purpose is to deceive the eye" (B. Baba Metziah 60a).

Note that the rabbis have a special name for this, *goneiv et ha-ayin*, "he steals the eye." In plain English this means deception.

Further in the above passage it says: "It is forbidden to paint man, or cattle, or utensils [to give them a younger or a new appearance]. This is obviously in the same category as our packaging and making an expensive cover for an inferior article.

The grosser forms of deception are naturally forbidden in a flat statement: "It is forbidden to deceive people in buying and selling or to deceive them by creating a false impression" (Maimonides, Mishneh Torah, Laws Concerning Sales, 18:1). This general statement is then spelled out in detail. "If one knows that an article that he is selling has a defect, he must inform the buyer about it."

From this we infer that if the seller does not specify any blemishes we may take it for granted that the article is in perfect condition. Maimonides rules therefore: "Whosoever buys an article without specifying any terms does so with the intention of buying an article that is free of defects. Even the seller specifies and explicitly says, 'I sell it on condition that you do not withdraw from the sale on the grounds of a defect in the article' the buyer may nevertheless withdraw, unless he waived his right after the seller specified the defect in the article before selling it or the buyer said he would accept the article that would reduce its value by so much and so much. Because he who forgoes the right to a claim, must know the amount of the claim he will forgo and explicitly specify it, just as one must specify in the case of overreaching."

Blackstone mentions the principle: *Sic utere tuo ut alienum non laedas* ("Use yours in such a manner that you do not harm another"). Salmond in his *Jurisprudence* says the following, however: "The landlord may intercept the access of light to his neighbors' windows, or withdraw, by means of excavation, the support which his land affords to his neighbor's house, or drain away the water which would otherwise supply his neighbor's well. His right to do all these things depends in no way on the motive for which he does them. The law cares nothing about whether his acts are inspired by an honest desire to improve his own property or by a malevolent impulse to damage that of others. He may do as he pleases with his own.

It should be mentioned that Roman law has a different ruling regarding the rights of adjoining proprietors. Harm done, *animo nocendi,* that is to say with malicious motive, was actionable (*Digest* 39.31.12). The German civil code, section 226, also provides quite generally that the exercise of a right is unlawful when its only motive is to harm another person.

What is the rabbinic rule regarding such cases? Again the law is very explicit. Maimonides following a ruling of the Talmud gives this rule: "If a man has a window in his wall, and another man comes and lays out a courtyard alongside of it, he cannot say to the owner of the window, 'Wall up this window so that you may not look into my property' inasmuch as the owner of the window has established his right to have his window open.

If, however, the other comes to build a wall over against the window in order to remove the discomfort caused by being exposed to the view of the owner of the window, he must build it at least four cubits away from the window in order not to obstruct the owner's light" (*Mishneh Torah* Laws Concerning Neighbors 7:1).

A similar example is the following: "One should not dig a cistern or a trench, or a vault, or draw a water canal, or make a pool wherein to soak and wash clothes near his neighbor's wall, unless it is three handbreadths away from it. And the wall of the cistern, or the pool, or the wall of the water canal which is on his neighbor's side must be plastered with lime in order to prevent the water from seeping through and damaging his neighbor's wall (ibid., 9:1).

A special instance where the ethics of the rabbis go far beyond the requirements of our law is the case of *dina d'bar metsrah,* which we translate as the law concerning the adjacent owner. We shall have to quote at length to illustrate this principle.

Thus Maimonides, following the Talmud, rules: "If one of the brothers or one of the joint owners of a plot of land sells his share to a stranger, the others may evict the purchaser, and the other brothers or joint owners pay him back the money that he gave in order that a stranger should not intrude between them. Moreover, if any man sells his land to another, the neighbor whose land is contiguous may pay the buyer the money he gave and evict him, and the distant buyer is considered as if he were the agent of the owner of the adjacent field.

This law of the adjacent owner applies, regardless of whether the other field is sold by the owner or by his agent or by the court. Even if the purchaser is a scholar, or a neighbor, or a relative of the seller, and the owner of the adjacent field is an unlearned person and not related to the seller, the latter nevertheless has priority and can evict the purchaser. This rule obtains because it is said, *And thou shalt do what is right and good* (Deuteronomy 4:18) and the Sages have held that since the sale is the same, it is *good* and *right* that this plot should be bought by the adjacent owner rather than one who has land at a distance" (*Mishneh Torah*, Laws Concerning Neighbors 12:4-5).

While the main thrust of our answer concerns itself with the legitimacy of manipulation, where the people who promote sales try to manipulate us through various devices and gimmicks, we must also take into account what the Talmud terms *geneivat da'at,* literally, the "stealing of the mind." It is a question whether we can include this in the realm of law. If law means regulations that can be enforced by the courts, then it is outside the legal realm. If law means rules of conduct we must follow even if these are not enforceable by the courts, then we are on solid ground. This stealing of the mind is, in plain English, creating a false impression. The Talmud enumerates instances which to us seem quite innocent, such as inviting a person to an affair because you know that he will not accept, and meeting someone casually on the street and telling him that you made this special trip just to meet him. But then the Talmud makes this categoric statement: "Just as the law against defrauding applies to buying and selling, so does it apply to defrauding by the spoken word. A man may not say, 'How much is the price of this item?' if he does not wish to buy it" (B. Baba Metzia 58b). Here the buyer creates a false impression, which the Talmud considers unethical. Our concern is more with the seller who tries to create a false impression by his packaging, by his methods of advertising, and by his marketing methods.

Our answer would then be that a person certainly has a right to sell his product, put it in the best light, give all its true virtues, and thereby make it attractive to the potential buyer. He may not, however, "manipulate" his customers, or use devices which, while not literally under the heading of fraud, do come under the guilt of "stealing the mind" by *suggestively* creating a false impression.

13. HATAFAT DAM (1970)

The social conditions affecting Jewish life and especially the Jewish family in America, have given new urgency to some old questions and created a host of new ones. The questions we shall deal with are in connection with *milah* (circumcision) and *hatafat dam* (the drawing of a drop of blood). The specific questions before us are:

QUESTIONS:
1. May a child born of a non-Jewish mother be circumcised *l'shem mitzvat milah* ("for the purpose of performing the mitzvah of circumcision," not just for surgical purposes)?
2. If the child is circumcised *l'shem mitzvat milah,* do we still require *hatafat dam*? If such a child were circumcised *kedat u-khedin* ("according to the requirements of the law"), but it was not done *l'shem giyur,* "for the purpose of conversion," do we take it into account when it is decided to have a conversion?
3. If it is known for sure that the child was circumcised not *l'shem mitzvah,* but rather for surgical reasons, will we need *hatafat dam* when and if the family decides to have the child converted?
4. If a child was circumcised before the eighth day, do we require *hatafat dam*?
5. In naming an adopted child when the natural mother is not Jewish and the child is therefore required to submit to conversion, do we insist on giving him the name, Avraham ben Avraham, as we do with adult converts, or may we use the adoptive father's name instead?

ANSWER: The talmudic source for this problem is the following passage:

> Rabbi Simeon ben Eleazar said: Beth Shammai and Beth Hillel did not differ concerning him who is born circumcised that you must cause a drop of blood to flow from him because it

94

is a suppressed foreskin; about what do they differ? About a proselyte who was converted when already circumcised; there Beth Shammai maintains, one must cause a drop of covenant blood to flow; whereas Beth Hillel rules: One need not cause a drop of covenant blood to flow from him (B. Shabbat 135a).

Tosafot calls attention to the fact that although from this passage it is quite obvious that a proselyte who has been circumcised before he converted does not require *hatafat dam*, all the authorities, with the exception of Rabbenu Hananel, maintain that *hatafat dam* is required. (Tosafot B. Shabbat 135a, s.v., *lo nehleku*, Tur, Rambam, RIF, *Halakhot Gedolot, Yoreh De'ah*, ROSH, Me'iri.)

To reconcile this discrepancy, *Tosafot* quotes the following passage in support of those who require *hatafat dam*. It reads as follows:

> For we have learned: If a person appeared and said, "I was circumcised but not immersed, let them immerse him, for what harm can it do?" So says R. Yehudah. R. Yosi says, "They do not immerse him" (B. Yebamot 46b).

The reason for R. Yosi's opinion is that the immersion must be preceded by *hatafat dam*. The same conclusion is drawn from another passage:

> May it be assumed that this is a question in dispute among Tannaim. A *mashukh* ("one who has drawn his foreskin so as to appear circumcised"), and one born circumcised, and a proselyte whose conversion took place while he was already circumcised . . . and all other circumcised persons . . . may be circumcised in daytime only. R. Eleazer ben Simeon, however, said: At the proper time children may be circumcised in the daytime only, and if not at the proper time, they may be circumcised both by day and by night (B. Yebamot 72a f.).

Both Rashi and Tosafot interpret the term, *V'ger shenitgayer k'she'hu ma'hul* ("and a proselyte who was converted while already circumcised") as referring to an Arab or a Gibeonite who were already circumcised but need *hatafat dam* in order to make the circumcision acceptable. (See Rashi ad loc., and Tosafot s.v. *d'Rabbi Yosi tarteh ba-i*, in B. Yebamot 46b).

These answers seem forced. After all the Talmud is very explicit when it says that the Bet Hillel maintain that no *hatafat dam* is required, and the final decision is always according to the Bet Hillel.

The parallel text in the Yerushalmi poses the same difficulty. The parallel text adds this conclusion:

> Rabbi Isaac b. Rabbi Nahman in the name of Rabbi Hoshayah said: The law is according to the disciple (P. Shabbat 19:2).

Who is the disciple referred to? The standard commentaries, Korban Ha'edah and P'nei Mosheh, both say that it refers to R. Simeon ben Eleazar who claims that according to the Bet Hillel no *hatafat dam* is required.

So far, the weight of talmudic evidence is still definitely in favor of maintaining that *hatafat dam* is not necessary. Why, then, do all the standard authorities disagree?

We must first check the claim of Tosafot that Rabbenu Hananel is of the opinion that a proselyte who was circumcised before he contemplated conversion does not need *hatafat dam* after conversion. In our printed text we have the following statement: *Ger shenitgayer keshehu mahul ein lo takkanah, aval hu be'atsmo lo.* If we translate this literally it reads as follows: "A proselyte who was converted when already circumcised, there is no remedy for him. But as for himself, no" (B. 135b). The last part of the statement is difficult to understand and the statement as a whole certainly does not bear out the claim of Tosafot. Professor Lieberman calls attention to Professor Aptowitzer's *Hosafot v'Tikunim l'RABYAH.* There, on page 54, is found a corrected text which reads as follows: *Ger shenitgayer keshehu mahul ein lo takkanah. Aval banav nimolin venikhnasin bekahal deha igayer betevilah u'khager hashuv lehakhshir zar'o, aval hu atsmo lo.* For this, the translation is: "A proselyte who was converted when already circumcised, there is no remedy for him. His sons, however, may be circumcised and may enter the congregation [of Israel] inasmuch as their father had converted by means of immersion, and he is accounted as a proselyte insofar as it makes his sons eligible but not himself." Evidently the copyist has skipped one or two lines. It would thus appear that Rabbenu Hanael rules that the children of a would-be proselyte who was circumcised before he contemplated conversion and did not submit to *hatafat dam* subsequently are full-fledged Jews. No *hatafat dam* was necessary to legitimatize his children.

The question that occurred to me immediately was, was his wife Jewish or not? If she was Jewish, then the children are Jewish regardless of his status. If she was not Jewish, then the children are not Jewish even if the father were a full-fledged Jew, let alone an incomplete proselyte. Checking in the Tur, I found that he paraphrased the text of Rabbenu Hananel as corrected in the RAVYAH, and found that the PERISHAH has already asked the question (*Tur Yoreh De'ah* 368) So did the TAZ. Their answer is that the mother was Jewish, but the *Hidush* here is that there is no stigma attached to the children that their father was Gentile. The immersion, even if there was no *hatafat dam*, gave him the status of a full proselyte for that purpose.

Professor Lieberman also calls attention to the She'iltot. There I found another authority who agrees with Rabbenu Hananel. In the commentary of the RI a Rabbenu Yeshayahu is quoted, and after arguing his case concludes: Therefore a proselyte who was circumcised while a Gentile does not need any *hatafat dam,* and needs only immersion (*tevilah*)" (She'iltot, beginning of parashah Vayera, Mirsky edition).

The answer to our main question is another reference given by Professor Lieberman. In answer to the question, Why do all the major authorities maintain a decision that is contrary to the explicit decisions of both the Babylonian and the Palestinian Talmud? Professor Lieberman's answer becomes an illustration of the adage, *Divrei Torah aniyim bimkomam ve'ashirim bemakam aher* ("The words of the Torah are poor in place and rich in another") by calling attention to a passage in the Midrash Rabba, of all places, which clears the question as if by magic. The passage reads as follows: After the statement of Rabbi Simeon ben Eleazar, as we have quoted it from the Talmud the Midrash adds:

> Rabbi Eleazar the son of Rabbi Eleazar Hakappar said: The Beth Shammai and the Beth Hillel do not differ in either case but agrees that the causing of a drop of blood to flow is required. Concerning what do they differ? Concerning a child that was born circumcised and the eighth day falls on a Sabbath" (B. Rabba 46:9, in the Theodor edition).

Here we have an explicit statement that a circumcised person who wants to convert is required to submit to *hatafat dam berit.*

Upon further study I found that the Gaon of Vilna in his commentary on the *Yoreh De'ah* 263:1, also quotes this Midrash, and a little further, in 265, subsection 66, calls attention to the fact that the *Sefer ha-Eshkol* has the text of the Midrash, and suggests that the same text should be adopted by the Palestinian Talmud. What we gain thereby is that the concluding statement of Rabbi Yitshak ben Nahman in the name of Rabbi Hoshaya to the effect that the law is according to the disciple, refers not to Rabbi Simeon ben Eleazar as the standard commentaries suggest, but to Rabbi Eleazar ben Rabbi Eleazar Hakappar who said that both the Bet Shammai and the Bet Hillel require *hatafat dam* for a circumcised Gentile who wishes to convert.

It is thus the accepted law that a would-be proselyte who was already circumcised, requires *hatafat dam* for conversion. *V'lulei demistephina* ("if I were not apprehensive") I would add that in the case of extreme emergency ("sha'at hadehak) we would permit him to be converted without *hatafat dam*. Such emergency cases are determined by medical and mental factors. The reason for this lenient measure is the following: According to the accepted norm, *hatafat dam* does not require a *berakha* ("blessing"). The commentators give the following reason for the rule. Since, according to the opinion of Rabbenu Hananel, that no *hatafat dam* is required, the performance of the ritual is based on a *safek* ("a doubt"), and we do not recite a *berakhah* on a *mitsvat safek*. By the same token we may say that *besha'at hadehak, ra'ui Rabbenu Hananel lismokh alav* ("Rabbenu Hananel is worthy that we rely upon him at least in case of emergency"). We venture this opinion *lehalakha* ("theoretically") but not *lema'aseh* ("as a decision to be applied") since the subject needs further study.

Ancillary to this question is the problem posed by a would-be proselyte who cannot submit to circumcision because of medical reasons. The sources discuss two analogous cases which may be adduced as supporting permission to convert in such cases without requiring circumcision:

a. A person whose brother died as a result of circumcision does not have to be circumsised (*Yoreh De'ah* 263:2).

b. If his *membrum* has been cut off, and thus he cannot be circumcised, it does not prevent him from converting, and immersion alone is sufficient (*Yoreh Deah* 265:1).

These instances indicate at least that there are circumstances where circumcision may be omitted without prejudicing the status of the person as a Jew. The authorities, however, with a few notable exceptions, invariably forbid conversion without circumcision no matter what the circumstances. Rabbi Yehiel Ya'akov Weinberg treats the case of a would-be convert who cannot be circumcised because of a cardiac condition. After a lengthy discussion he concludes that conversion cannot be permitted (*Sheilot u-Teshuvot Seridei Eish* vol. 2, no. 102). Rabbi Weinberg also cites a responsum of Rabbi Hayim Ozer Grodzinsky who reaches the same conclusion. Rabbi Kook, the first Chief Rabbi of Israel also has a responsum on the question and also forbids it (*Da'at Kohen*, sec. 106). The halakhic journal *Ha-Maor* of March 1964 has symposium on the question. Only Rabbi Zevi Cohen permits conversion. The others, Rabbi Mayer Amsel of New York, Rabbi Isaac Stern of Jerusalem, and Rabbi Ephrayim Greenblatt of Memphis, Tenn., all forbid it. Rabbi Zevi Charlap of Jerusalem also treats the question and reaches the same conclusion (*She'ilit u-Teshuvot Har Zevi, Yoreh De'ah*, no. 220). The only other exception is a teshuvah of Rabbi Hirshsprung of Montreal written to Rabbi Abraham N. Oler of Brooklyn, who was kind enough to send me a copy of it. It is to be noted that both rabbis who found a *heter* are functioning in Montreal. It is unlikely that this is a mere accident.

What about the case of *meitu ehav mahmat milah?* Today we would say that of a person who comes from a family of hemophiliacs and there is the danger of bleeding. Logically we cannot see any difference between this case and the previous one. There is, however, a *teshuvah* that treats this case specifically and reaches the conclusion that in such a case we permit conversion without circumcision (*She'ilot u-Teshuvot Imrei David*, no. 93). The major authorities, however, are so determined on this point that they forbid it even if the candidate for conversion is so eager that he is willing to risk the danger and to submit to circumcision.

There still is before us the question of whether a child born of a non-Jewish mother and who was circumcised properly, whom subsequently the parents decide to convert, is required to undergo *hatafat dam*?

In the circumcision of such a child there are three possibilities: a. The circumcision was merely surgical and without any religious significance. b. The circumcision was *l'shem mitzvat milah*, i.e., the parents, because of ignorance, believed that this was obligatory since the father was Jewish, and the *mohel* was unaware of the fact that the mother was not Jewish. c. The circumcision was the first step in the eventual conversion of the child. The officiant knew of the status of the child, and the parents had expressed a desire that the child be Jewish.

In the first case there is no doubt that *hatafat dam* is required. In the third case there is no question that *hatafat dam* is not required. The problem arises in the second case where the circumcision was performed *l'shem mitzvat milah*, but not *l'shem geirut*.

In the last case there is moreover the question of whether such a child may be ritually circumcised at all. Both the Tur and Rabbi Joseph Karo appear to imply that it is permitted, for they say: If an Israelite fathered a son by a heathen woman, the child may not be circumcised on the Sabbath. (Tur *Yoreh De'ah* 266; *Shulhan Arukh, Yoreh De'ah* 266:13). The Perishah, ad loc. however, adds: He may not be circumcised on a weekday either.

There is now a difference of opinion among the leading authorities on this question. Rabbi Yehiel Yaacov Weinberg forbids it categorically and actually issued on *issur* to the *mohalim* against performing such a circumcision. The reason he gives is that should we permit such a circumcision, these children might, as a result, be considered as full-fledged Jews even if there was no *tevilah* and no *giyur* at all. (*She'eilot u-Teshuvot Seridei Eish*, v. 2, responsa 95, 96). In addition, there is the danger that people will begin to believe that *milah* was sufficient for conversion contrary to the accepted norm that *mal v'lo toval k'ilu lo mal* ("If one was circumcised but did not immerse himself, it is as if he was not circumcised either"). This opinion is shared by Rabbi Azriel Hildesheimer (*She'eilot u-Teshuvot Rabbi Azriel,* responsa 229, 230), Rabbi Abraham Kook (*Da'at Kohen,* responsum 150), and Rabbi Hillel Posek (*She'eilot u-Teshuvot Hillel Omer, Yoreh De'ah,* responsum 128).

Alas, today when we are confronted with this question it is usually as a fait accompli; the child has already been circumcised and we are burdened with the task of finding out in what manner the circumcision was performed. For such a case we have the classic answer of Professor David Hoffman that even if the circumcision was done only *l'shem mitzvat milah*, no *hatafat dam* is required.

(See statement of Rabbi Morris Goodblatt on this question quoting *Melamed l'Ho'il Y. D.* responsum 82, and also *Noam*, vol 13, p. 38).

Rabbi Moshe Feinstein supports this ruling and adds that even if the *mohel* was under the misapprehension that the child was Jewish, no *hatafat dam* is necessary (*Igrot Moshe, Yoreh De'ah* responsum 48; and also *She'eilot u-Teshuvot Havalim Banimim,* v. 4, responsum 158; *She'eilot u-Teshuvot Peri Hasadeh,* v. 1. responsum 12). To go back to our question whether to circumcise such a child *lekhathilah.* We have sufficient authorities to permit it. Rabbi Goodblatt cites the Maharam Schick who permits it when both parents assent to it (*Yoreh De'ah* responsum 248) ; and Rabbi Judah Zirlsohn who also permits it (*She'eilot u-Teshuvot Atzei Levanon* responsum 64). One contemporary authority makes this recommendation to reconcile the conflicting opinions. Even those who ordinarily would forbid such a circumcision would permit it where the fathers show a desire to lead a Jewish life (see Rabbi Gedaliah Felder, *Nahalat Zevi,* v. 1,, p. 76).

We may thus conclude that if a circumcision was performed *l'shem mitzvat milah,* even if not *l'shem geirut,* no *hatafat dam* is required, because no *kavanah* that it be *l'shem geirut* is necessary (*Noam*, v. 13, p. 38). The only case where *hatafat dam* is necessary is where the circumcision was performed purely for surgical purposes. How can we tell? The authorities suggest that we judge according to how the circumcision was performed. (See Me'iri on Yebamot 46a). If a *mohel* performed the circumcision, it is reasonable to assume that it was performed *l'shem mitzvah.* Even if a physician performed it, and did it on the eighth day, recited the proper *berakhot,* and did it according to the halakhic prescription, it is counted as having been done *l'shem mitzvah.* We would thus conclude that if the circumcision was performed in a manner that we would also accept as *milah kesheirah,* we should also accept as having been performed *l'shem mitzvat milah* and not require *hatafat dam.*

The last question has no bearing on the subject of *hatafat dam;* it has the virtue of appearing with it. It is regarded as the custom to name a proselyte Avraham ben Avraham Avinu. This has called forth protests by the adoptive parents who would like to see the child they adopted bear their name and not the name of the natural parents, when the natural parent was Jewish, or ben Avraham Avinu, when the parent was not Jewish.

The objection to this request is that if we should give the child the name of the adoptive parents, it would not give the child's real identity and there is the worrisome possibility that he might marry a blood relative. Rabbi Moshe Feinstein discusses this question (*She'eilot u-Teshuvot, Igrot Moshe, Yoreh De'ah*, no. 161) and comes to the conclusion that this concern is very remote today. He, therefore, permits the child to bear the name of the adoptive father. As to the fear that people will not know that he is a proselyte, there is no reason to worry since there is a rule that at a certain stage of his development, the child must be told about his status in order that he should be able to revert back to the religion of his birth should he wish to do so, having been converted before he was in a position to give his consent. Rabbi Feinstein goes even further and suggests that although the practice is to give a name to the child after *tevilah*, if this causes embarrassment to the adoptive parents the name may be given at the circumcision (ibid).

Another question we wish to treat and which has become very common concerns the child that has been circumcised before the eighth day. This again is a new question caused by two new factors. It has become the custom to have the circumcision performed in a hospital. It has also become the custom in many localities to have the doctor perform it under the supervision of and in cooperation with the rabbi. Even if a professional *mohel* performs it, many parents wish that it be done in the hospital. When mothers who gave birth stayed in the hospital for at least two weeks, there was no problem, but now they are discharged before a week is over, circumcision would have to take place at home and doctors are not anxious to make house calls. They have, therefore, often performed the circumcision before the eighth day.

This practice is definitely forbidden and is termed *milah shelo b'zmanah* ("circumcision performed not at the proper time"). What if the question comes to us after such a circumcision was already performed, do we require *hatafat dam*?

The authorities are divided. In the *Shulhan Arukh* we have this ruling: "If a man transgressed and performed a circumcision at nighttime, he must return and cause a drop of covenant blood to come from him. If he performed the circumcision during the eight days, (i.e. before the eight day I. K.) but in the daytime, it is a valid circumcision." From this ruling it seems that *b'de'avad* it is *milah kesherah* ("valid circumcision") (*Yoreh De'ah* 262:1 in Ramo). Both the SHACH and the TAZ reject this opinion of the Ramo and require *hatafat dam* (ibid.). At the other extreme, is the ruling of the Sha'agat Aryeh to whom this is an invalid circumcision (*milah pesulah*) for which there is no remedy (*ein lo takkanah*) and the child retains the status of an uncircumcised person (*arel*). It is analogous to the case of one whose organ has been cut off.

The *Encyclopedia Talmudit* marshals a host of opinions on both sides, and, as is its policy, does not present any decision. We cannot afford this luxury and must come to a definite decision because the question comes up more and more frequently.

Since both, the SHACH and the TAZ and most of the later authorities (*Arukh ha-Shulhan Yoreh De'ah* 262:5; *Hakhmat Adam* 149:2) require *hatafat dam,* we should accept their opinion. We also have the additional reason to concur with them in order *l'migdar milta* ("to stem the tide of violation"). If we should not require *hatafat dam* when the violation of the biblical rule that circumcision be performed on the eighth day and not before will greatly increase. Since in this area we still have some power and jurisdiction we should exercise it. While these circumcisions are usually performed by a physician, the family also invites the rabbi to officiate with him. The rabbi should refuse to officiate at such a circumcision. If the doctor performs the circumcision by himself, without benefit of clergy, an unethical act if the family wants a religious and not a surgical act, the family usually comes to the synagogue at a later date to name the child at the services. *Hatafat dam* should be required before we permit it.

To sum up:

1. a child born of a non-Jewish mother may be circumcised;
2. if the child was circumcised *kedat u-khedin* even if not *l'shem geirut,* no *hatafat dam* is required for conversion;
3. if the circumcision was definitely surgical, *hatafat dam* is required before *tevilah,* if the child is to be converted;
4. in naming an adopted child, the adoptive father's name may be used, even if the child's natural parents are not Jewish;
5. if a child was circumcised before the eighth day, *hatafat dam* is required.

BIBLIOGRAPHY

Tosefta K'peshuta, Moed, Bi-ur Arukh, 253

Sefer Koret Habrit, Eliyahu Posek

Encyclopedia Talmudit, v. 9, under "Hatafat Dam"

Noam, v. 13, p. 31

Sefer ha-Eshkol, part 2. siman 38

Rabbinical Assembly Proceedings, 1941, p. 37

Rabbinical Assembly Law Committee Archives, especially statement
　　　　　on *hatafat dam* by Rabbi Morris Goodblatt and on the *ger*
　　　　　who is already circumcised, by Rabbi Eli Bohnen

She'eilot u-Teshuvot Sha'agat Aryeh, no. 52, 53, 54

She'eilot u-Teshuvot Melamed l'Hoil, part 2, no. 82

She'eilot u-Teshuvot Seridei Eish, part 2, No. 95, 96

She'eilot u-Teshuvot Rabbi Azriel, no. 229, 230

She'eilot u-Teshuvot Hillel Omer Yoreh De'ah no. 158

She'eilot u-Teshuvot Har Zevi v. 1. *Yoreh De'ah* no. 220

She'eilot u-Teshuvot Igrot Mosheh, Yoreh De'ah no. 158, 161

She'eilot u-Teshuvot Peri Hasadeh part 1, no. 12

She'eilot u-Teshuvot Havalim Banimim, v. 4, no. 36

She'eilot u-Teshuvot Maharam Schick, Yoreh De'ah n. 348

She'eilot u-Teshuvot Nahalat Zevi, Gedalish Felder, v. 1, p. 76

14. TAKKANOT (1973)

QUESTION: *What is the scope of takkanot and who has the power to enact them?*

ANSWER: The development and the widening of Halakha in order to find solutions to new problems created in the wake of new situations and new conditions, appeared in two forms: one came into being consciously and purposefully, and the other, unconsciously. By this we mean that our sages often created new laws without being aware of it. I am referring to the phenomenon of new laws coming into being in the schools of the sages, but the sages maintaining that they had not initiated anything new, that they were no innovators but merely interpreters; they simply revealed a new understanding that was latent in the words of the Torah. When they searched out some hint of support for their words in some explanation and interpretation of a certain biblical verse, a search which was ostensibly instituted only to find a reference to lean on and to reinforce their stand and give it the stamp of biblical authority, they claimed that, on the contrary, this was the genuine and actual meaning and that they merely called attention to what was already there (See Maimonides, *Sefer ha-Mitzvot*, root 2, and the strictures of Nahmanides thereto).

A parallel situation is to be found in the American and the British legal systems. Theoretically a judge has no legislative powers. Legislation is the province of the legislative department of the government. The judge merely interprets the existing laws or finds support for his verdict in a previous verdict that can serve as a precedent and as evidence for the validity of his decision. In reality, however, the decision is tantamount to new legislation. There is a difference of opinion among jurists whether in such instances the judge acts as a legislator or as an interpreter (see Justice Benjamin Cardoza, *The Nature of the Judicial Process*, chapter 3; and Rav Tza'ir, *Toldot ha-halakha*, part 1, p. 189).

In the case under our consideration, even in laws which the Talmud describes as *hararim hatluyim b's'ara* ("mountains hanging on a hair"), if one would have ventured to claim that the sages had initiated something new which was not already written in the Torah, they would have been astonished. If modern historians should claim there is new legislation here, the halakhist would counter that if there is, it was unintentional and the sages were not aware of it. (It is for this reason perhaps that the author of *Dorot ha-Rishonim* said, "During the whole gaonic period there was no legislation, and no *takkanot* were enacted and, during this long period of time, that of the gaonic period, stretching from 4349 to 4798, no general *takkanot* were enacted except two, i.e., that of *moredet* and that of the right to collect from movables" (*Dorot ha-Rishonim*, part 3, chapter 15). See comment of Rabbi Israel Shtsipansky on this ("Takkanot ha-Geonim," *Hadarom*, Tishri 5727, p. 135).

On the other hand, the Halakhah also grew and developed consciously and purposefully by means of *takkanot* and *gezeirot*. Maimonides, in his introduction to the Mishnah, defines these terms as follows: The laws that the prophets and the sages enacted in the last generations as a hedge around the Torah . . . and the sages call these *gezeirot*. The laws that were enacted by way of legislation and consensus in matters that obtain among people and which do not constitute an addition to the commandment or a reduction thereof, or in matters that will be of help to people in matters of Torah . . . this they call *takkanot* and *minhagim*.

Accordingly, *gezeira* is, substantially, the widening of the Halakhah as a hedge around the existing Halakhah. The purpose of *takkanah*, on the other hand, is either to legislate a new measure necessitated by a new situation because the existing Halakhah has no explicit answer or instruction concerning the problem, or to change the existing law which does not answer the demands of the current situation and the time has arrived to act for the public good, or to use the mishnaic term, for the sake of improving of the world (tikkum ho-olam).

History

According to the Talmud, the enactment of *takkanot* is a very ancient institution, and its roots date back to the very beginnings of the history of the Jewish people, as is well known. A number of *takkanot* are thus ascribed to Moses (Discussion of the Laws of Each Festival during the Festival (B. Megillah 32a) : reading the

Torah on Sabbaths, Festivals, Rosh Hodesh, the Intermediate Days
of the Festivals, etc. (P. Megillah 4:1; B. Baba Kamma 82a); the
last blessing of Birkat ha-Mazon (B. Berakhot 48b); that there be
eight divisions of *kohanim* who take turns at the Temple service
(B. Ta'anit 27a); seven days of feasting after the wedding of a
maiden, and seven days of mourning after the dead (P. Ketubbot
1:1 and B. Ketubbot 50a). We did not mention that the patriarchs
established the daily prayer of *Shaharit, Minhah* and *Ma'ariv* (B.
Berakhot 26b) because that is in the realm of Aggadat rather the
Halakha.

The following *takkanot* are ascribed to Joshua: Birkat ha-Aretz
(The second blessing of Birkat ha-Mazone—B. Berakhot 48a); the
ten conditions (or *Takkanot*) that Joshua stipulated to the children
of Israel when they entered Canaan (B. Baba Kamma 81a).

Boaz is given the credit for the *takkanah* that one should greet
his companion in the name of God (Mishnah Berakhot 9:5).

David enacted the *takkanot* raising the number of the divisions
of the *kohanim* to twenty-four (B. Ta'anit 27a), and that one must
recite a hundred blessings each day (B. Menahot 43b).

And so they ascribe *takkanot* to King Solomon, the prophets, and
to the men of the Great Synagogue, as is well known.

Even according to the modern historians the development of the
Oral Law was connected with the enactment of *takkanot* at the
very dawn of the history of the Halakhah. It is according to this
view that Zacharias Frankel, in his classical work *Darkhei ha-
Mishnah*, calls the early authorities of the Oral Law *Metaknei
Takkanot*—"enactors of *takkanot*." (Warsaw: 1923, p. 29. See also
Rav Tza'ir, *Toldot ha-Halakha*, part 1, pp. 197–254.

This process continued to our own day, especially now, in the
Holy Land, in connection with questions that were created by the
rise of the Jewish state and the in-gathering of the exiles.

Thus, although the enactment of *takkanot* has run an uninter-
rupted course in our history, we can still distinguish certain prominent and exceptional *takkanot* that appeared generally in times of
crisis, when it was necessary to reorganize the House of Israel in
order to adjust to new conditions and new situations, stand in the
breach against dangers that threatened the existence of the people
of Israel or a part of it. In this category we may mention:

The *takkanot* of Ezra and his court

The *takkanot* of Rabbi Yohanan ben Zaccai

The *takkanot* enacted at Usha

The *takkanot* of Rabbenu Gershom Ma'or Hagolah

The *takkanot* of Rashi and Rabbenu Tam

takkanot Shum (Speier, Worms, Mainz)

The *takkanot* of many individual communities

The *takkanot* of the Spanish exiles

The *takkanot* of the *Va'ad Arba ha'Aratzot*

The *takkanot* of the Survivors of the Holocaust (*She'eirit Hapleitah*)

The *takkanot* of the Israeli Chief Rabbinate

In addition to these which were actually series of *takkanot* enacted to meet current problems, there were individual *takkanot* usually ascribed to a single authority but actually the product of his school or synod or court. The best known example is the *prosbal* (Greek, "for the court"), described as a *takkanah* of Hillel but that must have been enacted by his school as a whole or the panel of the court over which he presided.

One more aspect that we must note is the fact that these *takkanot* were enacted for *k'lal Yisro'el*, the total Jewish community. Many of them, however, were intended for a specific community and for a specific time. And yet even of these *takkanot* originally intended for a specific locale and for a limited time, many spread beyond the geographic bounds for which they were intended and beyond the specific time; and with the passage of time they were accepted by *k'lal Yisroel* as an established law. An example of this is the *herem* of Rabbenu Gershom against polygamy.

From time to time, great spiritual leaders arose who bridged the boundaries between one spiritual center and another. Generally, however, each autonomous center turned to its own halakhic authorities with its questions, and there was no central authority to issue orders that would command the respect and observance of all the diaspora (Rabbi Israel Shtzipansky, "*Takkanot ha-Rishonim*," *Hadarom*, Tishri 5729 p. 145; Menahem Elon, *Mavo L'mishpat ha'Ivri* p. 547).

The Power to Enact *Takkanot*

The central issue in the subject of *takkanot* is, who has the power and the authority to enact *takkanot*? According to Maimonides, it

is the High Court in Jerusalem that is the basis of the Oral Law
and hence issues laws and ordinances to all the people of Israel
(Maimonides, *Mishneh Torah,* Laws Concerning Apostates 1:1).

When does this apply, however? In normal times, when there was
a central authority with power to legally compel the entire community. Here, we do not take into account the *takkanot* ascribed
to Moses, Joshua, David, Solomon, and the prophets. We must start
with Ezra and his court. We may say that Maimonides did not refer
specifically to the High Court of Jerusalem, but rather to any place
where the High Court might have been located at that time, such
as Yavneh or Usha; and not necessarily in the Land of Israel, but
anytime and anyplace that the Jewish people had established a
central authority that was recognized by all. The *bet din* of that
place had the power to enact *takkanot,* and the imprimatur of that
central authority was sufficient for the *takkanah* to be accepted by
k'lal Yisroel. Although, theoretically, there was the problem of the
validity of the *semikha* of these authorities of the diaspora, in reality
their legal activities were authoritative and binding; and though
they did not issue from Jerusalem, the legislation knew no territorial boundaries (see RDBZ ad loc., who does differentiate between
the High Court of Jerusalem and the *bet din* at Yavneh, based on
the comment of the *Sifrei* on the verse: And thou shalt do according
to the tenor of the sentence, which they shall declare unto thee from
that place which the Lord shall choose (Deuteronomy 17:10) that
only the violation of instructions emanating from the High Court
of Jerusalem incurs the penalty of death, but there is no penalty of
death in the case of rules emanating from Yavneh).

Since the end of the geonic period, the legislation which, until
now, was for *k'lal Yisroel* assumed a local character, i.e. several
centers arose and each had authority over that center alone (Elon,
M., *Mavo,* p. 547, R. Israel Shtzipansky, "Takkanot Shum," *Hadarom,* Tishri 5728 p. 173). With the decline of the Babylonian center at the end of the geonic period, the situation changed because
the spiritual center moved to Europe and North Africa, and the
change was not from one center to another that assumed the
hegemony, but rather to several smaller centers which arose simul-
taneously and functioned one beside the other without one achieving
authority over the others. Many communities arose in the various
cities of Europe and the organized community (*kehilah*), or an

organization of several communities and, sometimes, even more inclusive and larger bodies, became an autonomous independent center. Alongside such centers in the countries of North Africa there arose similar centers in Germany, Spain, France, Italy, Turkey, the Balkan countries, Poland, Lithuania, and others (Elon, *Mavo*, p. 547).

In the Europe of the Middle Ages, therefore, the enactment of *takkanot* was in the hands of rabbinic synods that gathered specifically for such purposes. During the later Middle Ages the most important promulgators of *takkanot* were the representatives of the *kehilot* who established these *takkanot* to strengthen and improve the structure of the *kehilot*.

These *takkanot*, as we have said, were established by the officials of the *kehilah* and its representative members (*Tovei Ha'ir*). The basis of the *takkanot* was the Halakhah, and the *takkanot* had to be validated by the rabbis. We have a rich literature on this period, on the *kehilot* and on the *takkanot* they had enacted (Dr. Louis Finkelstein, *Jewish Self-Government in the Middle Ages*, N.Y. 1924; R. Israel Shtzipansky, *Hadarom*, nos. 22, 24, 26, 28; *Ha-Onshim ahar Hati'mat Hatalmud*, Harav Simha Asaf, Jerusalem 5682; *Takkanot Medinat Maeren*, Y. Heilperin, Jerusalem 5702; *Takkanot Nikolsburg*, A.N.Z. Roth, Sura edition, 5722; *Sefer Takkanot Kandia*, A.S. Hartum and M.Z.A. Kasuto, Jerusalem 5703; *Takkanot Kahal Pozna v'ha-Medina*, Dr. L. Levin, Frankfurt-a-M.: 1926; *Pincas va-ad Arba ha-Aratzot*, Y. Heilperin, Jerusalem: 5705; *Pinkas Va'ad Medinat Lita*, S. Dubnow, Berlin: 5685; *Sefer Hatakkanot, Minhagei Yerushalayim*, Ya'akov Sha'ul, Yerushalayim: 5643; *Sefer Eretz ha-Hayim, Dinim Uminhagim v'takkanot b'Eretz Yisrael*, Hayim Sithon, Safed: 5669, "*Lemahutan shel Takkanot Hakahal Ba-Mishpat ha-Ivri*," M. Elon in *Mehkeri Mishpat l'zekher Avraham Rosenthal*, pp. 1–54, Jerusalem: 5724; "*Ha-Ikronot ha-Halakhati'yim ha-Mishpatiyim she'Aleihem Mushtatot Takkanot Hakehilot*," Shelomo-Tal, in *Dinei Yisroel, Shenaton ha-Mishpat ha-Ivri v'eledinei Mishpaha b'Yisroel*, v. 3, pp. 31–60.)

A good summary of the subject of who has the power and the authority to enact such *takkanot* with normative force, is found in the *Responsa* of Rabbi Eliyahu Mizrahi. According to his opinion, if there is agreement among the great authorities of each generation (*gedolei ha-Dor*) they have the power and the authority

ascribed to the High Court of Jerusalem. He found support for this
stand in the well-known talmudic statement that Jephthah, in his
generation, had the same authority as the Prophet Samuel in his
generation, or Jeruba'al in his generation (B. Rosh Hashanah 25b).
The *Hazon Ish* maintains that the rulings of the scholars of each
generation are as binding as the *takkanot* of the sages of the Talmud
(Eben ha-Ezer, 63 subsec. 7, quoted in *Torah Sh'ba'al Peh* 5730, p.
49, by Dr. Yitshak Kister).

And what about great scholars (*gedolei ha-Torah*) found in individual communities whose authority is limited to that individual
community? On this there is a difference of opinion between the
authorities. Maimonides, Rabbenu Tam, the Rosh, and the Tur
maintain that the power to enact *takkanot* was granted only to the
great scholars of each community (*gedolei ha-kehilah*); Rashi, Rav-
Yah, and the Rashba maintain that the power was conferred as
well on scholars whose authority was accepted only in their individual communities. Which of those opinions was accepted and pre-
vailed in *k'lal Yisroel* we may learn from the many local *takkanot*
which were originally intended to be only local and then assumed
the authority of a law that was normative for *k'lal Yisroel*. (See,
Seider Kidushin u'Nesuin of A. H. Freiman who deals at length
with such *takkanot* that dealt with divorce and marriage.)

Since the end of the eighteenth century, from the coming of
Emancipation, the autonomous body of a living and vigorous community which had the power of legislation and sanction became a
weak organism without initiative or vision, without any creative or
developmental function in the legal area. The causes for this were
twofold: external, because of the loss of communal autonomy and
removal from the Jewish court (*bet din*) of any coercive powers;
and internal, the gradual division of the community into traditional
and nontraditional groups, and the concommitent loss of inner religious discipline regulated by the Jewish court (see, *"L'Mahutan
shel Takkanot ha-Kahal,* M. Elon, *Mehkerei Mishpat lezehker Avraham Rosenthal,* p. 2, note 9).

Limits

It is stated in the Mishnah, repeated in the Gemara, and then
presented in the codes that a limit was set to the power of the
enactment of *takkanot*. Thus they said: "No court may set aside

the decision of another court unless it is greater in wisdom and in numbers" ('Eduyot 1:5). "We should not impose a restriction upon a community unless the majority of the community will be able to stand it" (B. Baba Kamma 79b). "A *bet din* cannot lay down a condition which would cause the abrogation of a law of the Torah" (B. Yebamot 89b). On the other hand, it does state: With an abstention from the performance of an act it is different—"*sheiv v'al Ta'aseh sha'anei*" (B. Yebamot 90a Gittin 36b), i.e., in a case like this, when being passive causes the abrogation of a law of the Torah, we permit it (sit still and do nothing).

"Rabbi Eleazar ben Jacob stated: "I heard that even without any Torah'itic ruling authority, the *bet din* may administer flogging and death penalties; not, however, for the purpose of transgressing the words of the Torah but in order to make a fence for the Torah" (B. Yebamot 90b).

Maimonides, in The Laws Concerning Apostates (*Mamrim*) explains and extends these principles as follows:

a. The *bet din* may abrogate a law of the Torah if it is a temporary measure (2:4). Maimonides gives a rationale for this, as is his wont, as follows: "Even as a physician will amputate the hand or the foot of a patient in order to save his life, so the court may, when an emergency arises, advocate the temporary disregard of some of the commandments, so that the commandments as a whole may be preserved. This is in keeping with what the early sages said: 'Desecrate on his account one Sabbath that he may be able to observe many Sabbaths' " (*Mishneh Torah*, Laws Concerning Apostates, 2:4; see also B. Yoma 85b).

b. No *takkanot* may be enacted except to safeguard the law (ibid.)

c. If a court decreed a preventive measure or instituted a *takkanah* . . . and another court that succeeded it wished to rescind the measure of the earlier court and to abolish that *takkanah* . . . it is not empowered to do so unless it is greater than it in wisdom and in numbers (*Mishneh Torah*, Laws Concerning Apostates 4:3).

d. And this is only if these measures were universally accepted among the people of Israel. If a measure is not universally accepted, there is no need to have a court that is superior in wisdom and in numbers to rescind it. If a matter, decreed to serve as a protective fence around the law, has been universally accepted among the people of Israel, no later court, even if it is superior to the former, is enpowered to abrogate it or permit it (ibid.).

e. Even if the cause for which the measure was decreed or the *takkanah* enacted has ceased to exist, the court may not later abolish these laws unless it is superior to the earlier court (*Mishneh Torah*, Laws Concerning Apostates 4:2).

f. Before instituting a decree or enacting a *takkanah* or introducing a custom that it deems necessary, the court should calmly deliberate the matter and make sure that the majority of the community can live up to it. At no time is a decree to be imposed upon the public which the majority cannot endure (*Mishneh Torah*, Laws Concerning Apostates 4:5).

And the Meiri said: "We have already explained in our Mishnah that a *bet din* cannot lay down a condition which would cause the abrogation of a law of the Torah, except in one of the following ways: either in a case of abstention from the performance of an act (*sheiv v'al ta'aseh*), or a case of declaring money (or its equivalent) as ownerless (*hefker*), or if it is a temporary measure as a fence and protective wall around the Torah. In any case, in the whole matter of marriage no abrogation is involved since whosoever espouses (*mekadeish*) does so according to the provision of the rabbis and they therefore are empowered to amend the espousal (Meiri, *Yebamot* p. 330, Berlin, 5682)

Generally the *takkanot* were a form of legislation that purported to solve new problems resulting from changes in the social, economic, and moral process of the public and the individual, to fill what was lacking, and to repair what needed repairing—but obviously without any conflict with the existing laws:—but if there is such a conflict, the above-mentioned principles must be observed.

The Purpose of the *Takkanot*

From what we already said it is understood that *takkanot* were enacted in order to repair what was impaired or to use the talmudic expression to erect a protecting fence or hedge around the existing law. There were, however, other motives that served as an impetus for the enactment of *takkanot*:

1. In the interests of peace (*mipnei darkhei shalom*). "A *kohen* is called up first to read the Torah, and after him a Levite, and then a lay Israelite, in the interests of peace" (Mishnah Gittin 5:7).

2. For the good order of the world (*mipnei tikkun ha'olam*), i.e., to prevent abuses. "Neither should scrolls of the Torah, phylacteries, and *mezuzot* be bought from heathens at more than their value, to prevent abuses" (Gittin 4:6).

3. To help penitents (*mipnei takkanat hashavim*): If a beam which had been wrongfully appropriated is built into a palace, restitution for it may be made in money (instead of restoring the actual beam) (Mishnah Gittin 5:5).

4. To help the market (*takkanat hashuk*): Biblically speaking, the delivery of money effects the transfer of title. Why then was it said that only drawing (*meshikhah*) gives possession? As a precautionary measure, lest he say to him, "Your wheat was burnt in the loft" (B. Baba Metsia 46b).

5. To prevent shutting the door to borrowers: The *prosbol* (Mishnah Shebi'it 10:4, Gittin 4:3).

We must call your attention here to the confusion in the cases mentioned in the use of the word *takkanah;* one usage is to improve a situation, as Tikkun ha-Olam, and the other is legislation; but this is not the place to expatiate on the subject.

After the close of the Talmud, especially after the end of the geonic period, the period of *takkanot* of individual communities blossomed forth. The change in conditions and in the standings of the *bet din* gave impetus to a new type of *takkanah*, that of strengthening discipline in the community and firming up the institutions of the kehilah, as we have already mentioned above.

In our own days, the most important *takkanot* were concerned with allowing the *agunot* resulting from the war (wives of soldiers) and the survivors of the holocaust to remarry. For example: In the summer of the year 5705, between the 17th of Tamuz and Tisha B'Av, the rabbis of Romania, in the city of Arad, formerly part of Hungary, gathered to take counsel regarding aid for the *agunot* of the surviving remnant saved from the holocaust, and to permit the remarriage of *agunot* whose husbands were murdered in the holocaust (*She'eilot u-Teshuvot Minhat Yitshak*, part 1, no. 1; see also, *Otzar Ha-Posekim*, v. 7; Sec., on the *agunot* of the holocaust, *She'eilot u-Teshuvot Tzitz Eliezer*, v. 3, no. 25; *She'eilot u-Teshuvot Heikhal Yitshak*, Rabbi Isaac Herzog, part 2, devoted entirely to the problem). In Jerusalem during World War II there was a center

for freeing *agunot* resulting from the war from their plight. (Sefer
Ha'Agunot, Kahana, p. 57)

Even though the above treatises do not really have *takkanot* in
the legislative sense, but are, rather, a clarification of the law as it
applied to the problem, there is no doubt that many of these partake
of the nature of *takkanot*. If there is any doubt as to whether these
takkanot agunot were actually *takkanot* (rather than efforts to
help), there is no such doubt that what has transpired in the central Bet Din of Israel and at the conferences gathered at the initiative of the Chief Rabbinate, have all the earmarks of *takkanot*.
This is not the place to expatiate on the many legal enactments that
were instituted officially in areas which the government had assigned to the jurisdiction of the Chief Rabbinate and the rabbinic
courts. These Takkanot are the fruit of the in-gathering of the
exiles (*kibbutz galugot*) See, *"Nimukei Hatakkanot Shenit'hadshu
b'veit Midrashah shel ha-Rabbanut Harashit shel Eretz Yisroel,"
Talpiyot*, Tishri 5705, p. 457; Menahem Elon, *Hahakikah Hadatit
b'Yisroel*).

Summing Up

Maimonides ruled: A *bet din* has the power to abrogate *takkanot*
temporarily even if it is inferior to the earlier authorities, so that
these decrees be not more stringent than the words of the Torah
itself, seeing that each *bet din* has the power to abrogate these
rulings temporarily (Mishneh Torah, Laws Concerning Apostates
2:4).

In an old book dealing with the *takkanot* of Jerusalem that has
been reprinted recently, I found the statement: "From all that has
been said above we can infer that a *bet din* has the power to enact
takkanot according to the needs of the time and season, even if it
means the abrogation of a matter decreed in the Torah" (*Sefer
ha-Takkanot u'Minhagim*, Ya'acov Sha'ul Elyashar, Jerusalem:
5642, photographed edition 5729).

To be sure the *posekim* and *batei din* of each generation en-
deavored with all the means at their disposal not to abrogate any
law of the Torah, and not to rule contrary to the accepted practice.
Therefore, even when it was obvious that the *takkanah* under consideration was contrary to the accepted Halakhah, scholars searched
hard for some reasoning that would conciliate the two. Thus, in

money matters they saw no obstacle to any new ruling no matter how much it was counter to the accepted ruling on the principle of *hefker bet din hefker* ("the *bet din* has the right to declare any possession ownerless"). In the laws of marriage, also, when they declared a marriage void they did it on the claim that whosoever weds (*kal demekadeish*), does so according to the ruling of the rabbis. In addition to this they explained in many instances that where it means abstention from an act, the ruling is different. Basically, however, they did not hesitate to enact *takkanot* when necessary, even where those claims did not apply.

There is no doubt that we live in an era that is crucial in regard to halakkic legislation. First, dealing with the diaspora, alas there is no kehila that has the authority to legislate or that has any coercive powers. Other institutions have been established to fill the gap. Instead of kehilot we have national synagogue organizations and national rabbinic bodies the aim of which is to bring some order and discipline at least into these areas of Jewish life. We have to admit to our sorrow that these are more often signs of weakness and fragmentation than signs of strength and centralization, signs of territorial as well as ideologic fragmentations. Instead of improving the situation, they often make the crisis more conspicuous. In America, today, there are five Orthodox rabbinic organizations; among the Conservative and Reform groups there are left wings, right wings, and centers; in the lay organizations the situation is analogous. As for the concept of a kehila, there is not today in the diaspora a body with authority and coercive power even for a small segment of the house of Israel.

In spite of that, we are not among the "negators of the *galut*" if that means that outside the Land of Israel there is no possibility of establishing a truly Jewish community dedicated to Torah. We believe that the talmudic adage, "Wherever the Children of Israel were exiled the *Shekhina* went with them" is true even today. We also believe that today, too, it is possible to establish a place for Torah to flourish, and to raise scholars even in the diaspora, especially in America. We also believe, however, that with the reestablishment of the State of Israel, this will be the only place where a *possibility* to enact *takkanot* in the old accepted sense will be possible, i.e., that there will be the authority of a center recognized by *k'lal Yisroel*. This would strengthen the authority of

Halakhah not only in Israel. In the diaspora the house of Israel is breached, and its walls, so to say, are in ruins. The influence of the rabbis is great, but their authority is insignificant. Even if they should enact *takkanot*, they would operate in a vacuum.

And this brings with it another drawback. I remember reading the autobiography of Rabbi Meir Berlin (Later Bar-Ilan) *Fun Volozhin biz Yerushalayim"* and he called attention to this phenomenon. The rabbis of Odessa, a city known for its lack of religious observance, were stricter in their decisions on religious matters than the rabbis of Kovno and Vilna. He explained it thusly: This was not due to the fact that the rabbis of Odessa were more scrupulous about religious observance, but rather the opposite. In Kovno and Vilna the Jews abided by the decisions of the rabbis and therefore the rabbis had the responsibility of dealing with these questions as relevant to daily life and not as a theoretical matter. In Odessa they did not pay attention to the rabbis, hence they could afford to be strict—since it made no practical difference—and they could feel most pious and concerned. The analogy to America is quite obvious.

To be sure, this does not exempt us from the warning implied in the following passage of the Talmud: "My people ask counsel of their stock and their staff (*makkelo*) declareth unto them (Hosea 4:12), whosoever is lenient (*mekal*) to him he concedes (Pesahim 52b)" (This is a humorous play on words connecting *makkel,* a staff, with *mekal,* he is lenient).

At the end of World War II, I had the privilege to be the first American soldier to enter Amsterdam, the metropolis of Holland, and to free Rabbi Justus Tal who later became the Chief Rabbi of Holland. He was among the *mahmirim*. In a conversation with him on a halakhic matter he quoted his teacher to the effect that today we should add two new *al Hets* to the already long list recited on Yom Kippur; *al het shehatanu lefanekha b'v'hai bahem v'lo sheyamot bahem,* and, *al het shehatanu lefanekha b'mutav sheyehyn shogegin v'al yihyu mazidin.* Truthfully, this is a genuine anxiety that on the basis of these talmudic adages we will allow many lapses in religious observance. However, we counter, as the Talmud often does, *atu b'shuftinei askinan?* (B. Baba Batra 122a)—"are we dealing with lawbreakers?" We are dealing now with responsible people, distinguished representatives of the community, whose sincere desire is to provide for the welfare of the community and to strengthen the influence of the Torah.

There is a general consensus to pin our hope on a central halakhic establishment in Israel with authority and prestige. Even in the days when the majority of the great scholars were in the diaspora, the courts of the land of Israel enjoyed a priority due to the favored position it held in the hearts of the people, as is told in the Jerusalem Talmud. Commenting on the verse "unto the residue of the elders of the captivity" (Jeremiah 29:1), "The Holy One blessed be He said: Exceeding beloved are to me the elders of the captivity, but even more beloved is to me a small group in the Land of Israel than the Great Sanhedrin outside of the Land of Israel (Nedarim 6:9). How much more so today, when we are witnessing the realization of the prophecy, "For out of Zion shall go forth the Torah and the word of the Lord from Jerusalem" (Isaiah 2:3). Where else could the preamble of a *takkanah* be worded in this fashion:

> Because of the in-gathering of the exiles from the widespread areas of the Golah, from the ends of the earth and the distant islands whence come the thousands and the tens of thousands, and because of the abundant kindness of the Lord to us, settled here, and because they bring with them ancient *minhagim* that do not fit the *takkanot* of the sages, the masters of the Land of Israel who are in Jerusalem, the Holy City may it be rebuilt soon, the *takkanot* of the rabbis of the kehilot in Israel, enacted in matters of divorce and marriage, levirate marriage, and *halisa,* which are bound to cause dissension in Israel and destroy the peace of the House of Israel, For this reason we found it necessary and considered it our obligation to renew the *takkanot* of our ancient rabbis of blessed memory, and to add similar *takkanot* which the times demand for the sake of the ways of peace and the peace of the House of Israel which are the basic premises for all the *takkanot* of our ancient rabbis from the days of Moses until the latest generations, in their respective *kehilot.*

With the permission of the Holy One blessed be He and His *Shekhina,* and with the permission of the *Bet Din shel Ma'alah* and the *Bet Din shel Matah,* and with the consent of the ancient rabbis, masters of the Land of Israel, and with the consent of the distinguished excellencies (*geonim*) members of the enlarged advisory body of the Chief Rabbinate, we decree and enact with the authorization of our Holy Torah, as were all *takkanot*, the *takkanot* of (the house of) Israel that were promulgated among the People of Israel, in their respective *kehilot*, for all the generations to come (Preamble to the Takkanot of the Chief Rabbinate of Israel at a national conference of rabbis, held in Jerusalem, 17–21st of Shevat 5710).

Since the days of the geonim of Babylonia it was not possible to use such strong and authoritative language to address *k'lal Yisroel*. On the one hand we exclaim, Happy is the generation that had the *Zekhiya* for this. On the other hand we wail. Woe unto the generation that will not exploit this opportunity of establishing a central authoritative institution with authority and prestige that will be recognized in all Jewish communities.

Alas the time for it has not arrived yet. The central authority, instead of having the vision and the wisdom to unite the religious house of Israel has become a stumbling block, an expression of party politics, with sectarian tendencies. We are, therefore, still at the stage where the right to enact *takkanot* is exercised by individual groups and localities.

It is our prayer that eventually the love for Israel and the Torah of Israel will find a way of establishing unity at least in certain areas, so that in these we shall be able to act for *k'lal Yisroel*. *Yehi ratzon, shenizkeh v'nihyeh, uenireh.*

15. QUESTIONS RABBIS ASK

QUESTION: *What is to be done with amputated limbs of Jewish patients? Is it permissible to burn tissue after examination?*

ANSWER: The answer to this question depends upon whether the obligation of burial applies only to the body of a deceased person or also to amputated limbs. It is interesting to note that in the *Ethical and Religious Directives for Catholic Hospitals* issued by the Catholic Hospital Association, under Disposal of Amputated Members it says: "Major parts of the body should be buried in the cemetery when it is reasonably possible to do so. Moreover, the members of Catholics should, if possible, be buried in blessed ground. When burial is not reasonably possible, the burning of such members is permissible."

The rabbinic authorities have involved in this question the problem of *tumat kohen*. Where that is not involved, the general opinion is that *kevurah* (burial) does not apply to limbs, and hence there is no objection to incineration. See:

> She'eilot u-Teshuvot Melamed L'ho'il, Part 2, No. 118
> She'eilot u-Teshuvot Shevut Ya'akov Part 2, No. 101
> She'eilot u-Teshuvot Noda b'Yehudah, Mehadura Tinyana, Yoreh De'ah, no. 209
> She'eilot u-Teshuvot Maharil Diskin
> Sefer Doveir Shalom, part 1, Shlomo Zer-Tovim (5733)

QUESTION: *Should a boy without fingers on his left hand put the tephilin on his right arm, or just skip the part done on the fingers?*

ANSWER: The *Shulhan Arukh* rules: An amputee who has no hand, only his arm should put the *tephilin* on it without reciting the blessing. (Oreh Hayim 27:1). This is based on a talmudic statement (B. Menahot 37a) which Tosafot (s.v., *Kiboret*) interprets that as long as the amputation is not beyond the elbow, the obligation to put the *tephilin* on it still obtains. The *Mishnah Berurah* says explicitly about the word of the *Shulhan Arukh*, "who has no hand," that it means that his hand proper with the ulna up to the elbow. If, however, part of the ulna was left all the authorities agree that he is to put on the *tephilin*—with a blessing (Oreh Hayim 27: in *Mishnah Berurah* subsec. 5). Hence, the answer is that boy proceeds as a normal boy would, but skips the twining of the *retzuah* over the missing fingers.

QUESTION: *What should patients who are on a salt-free diet do about salting meat?*

ANSWER: Methods of salting meat have been suggested by Dr. Bruno Kisch and Dr. Macht (the late, renowned pious scientists of Baltimore, Md.) They are very involved and quite burdensome. Furthermore, I showed the process to a physician who commented that anybody who eats such meat after it has undergone this process has to be starving first. Since the people who are on a salt-free or salt-poor diet are under this restriction because of the sodium content of the salt (the Na in NaCl), I inquired whether there are salts without sodium and whether they have the same effect as ordinary salt as far as drawing the blood from the meat is concerned but is not injurious to the heart. I was told that potassium chloride is such a salt and it is slightly more expensive than regular salt.

QUESTION: *When a* brit *occurs on Shabbat, may the* mohel *ride to the circumcision, or should it be postponed until the next day?*

ANSWER: The question did not mention the third alternative, that of the *mohel* spending Shabbat near where the circumcision will take place (*Arukh ha-Shulhan Yoreh De'ah* 266:5) Evidently it is a case where this alternative is not feasible. What then? Should we say that in this case the principle of *milah dohah Shabbat* ("the *mitzvah* of circumcision supersedes the observance of the Shabbat") applies and we should permit the *mohel* to travel, in order to have *milah b'zmanah*? or should we postpone the circumcision, as we do in other cases (see *Ot Shalom* subsec. 6, for other instances where postponement may be advocated).

There are other practical considerations. With the new epidemic of *milah shelo b'zmanah* ("circumcisions performed before the eighth day"), it may be necessary to insist that it be on the eighth day no matter what. Furthermore, if we permit postponement we shall find ourselves having every *brit* on a Sunday. On the other hand, where the fear of *hilul Shabbat* not only on the part of the *mohel* but also by the other participants is very real, postponement may be the wiser choice. Hence, each case has to be judged individually. (See, *She'eilot u-Teshuvot Melameid L'Hoil Y.D.* no. 80; *Sedeh Hemed*, letter *mem*, Sec. 86, s.v., *v'im Mumar l'halel Shabatot; She'eilot u-Teshuvot Igrot Moshe, Yoreh De'ah* 156; Rabbi Simon Schwartz in *Hapardes;* Tishri 5732; Rabbi Bunim Pirsutzky, *Hapardes*, Kislev 5732.

QUESTION: *May a convert say Kaddish after his father who is a Christian. May a Jew say Kaddish after his father who is a mumar?*

ANSWER: Theoretically a proselyte is like a new-born child (B. Yebamot 48b) who has no kin and therefore no obligation to those who were his kin before his conversion. The authorities however permit him to say *Kaddish*, and some even claim that it is his obligation to do so, whether the *Kaddish* effects a *tikkun* for the soul of the deceased or is an affirmation of faith there can be no objection. Today, when the bonds of love for family are not severed, there certainly can be no objection. (See, on the subject: *Leket Hakemah Hahadash*, O.H., Secs. 46-87: *Dinei Kaddish*, p. 316, subsec. 78. *She'eilot u-Teshuvot Zekan Aharon*, R. Aaron Walkin v.2., Yoreh De'ah no. 87; *Mimama'akim*, R. Efrayim Oshri v. 3 no. 5).

QUESTION: *May a rabbi officiate at a funeral where the body will be cremated?*

ANSWER: The Jewish way of burial has been to place the body in the earth, hence, cremation is frowned upon. The questions that arise on cremation are:
1. May the ashes be buried in the congregational cemetery?
2. Should a rabbi officiate at such a funeral?
A large number of authorities forbid the burial of the ashes in a Jewish cemetery because that will encourage the practice of cremation (See, *Duda'ei Hasadeh*, no. 16; *Shei'eilot u-Teshuvot Mahaneh Abraham*, part 2, *Yoreh De'ah*, no. 38; and *Hayei Olam* by R. Meir Lerner). Others permit the burial, and even permit a service at the burial (Rules of the Burial Society of the United Synagogue of London, quoted in a *Guide to Life* by Rabbi H. Rabinowitz, p. 29).

The practice approved by the Rabbinical Assembly Law Committee is as follows:

Cremation is forbidden when it is done by the family in disregard of Jewish practice. The rabbi may officiate at a service in the funeral parlor only. The ashes may be buried in a Jewish cemetery, and appropriate prayers may be recited, but not by the rabbi lest it be construed as approval. (*Proceedings of the Rabbinical Assembly*, 1939, p. 156; *Archives of the Rabbinical Assembly Law Committee*).

QUESTION: *Are turbot, lumpfish, and mahi-mahi kosher fish?*

ANSWER: The requirements for considering a fish kosher have been given above in the *teshuvah* on swordfish. We have now to ascertain whether these fish satisfy the requirements.

Turbot is of the family teleosts to which belong most of the kosher fish. In the *Fishery Leaflet 531* issued by the Bureau of Fisheries it is listed as a kosher fish. It is so because it is covered with cycloid scales. (Prof. Carl Gans, Chairman, Department of Zoology, University of Michigan). Hence we consider turbot kosher.

Lumpfish. In *Fishes of the Atlantic Coast of Canada*, by A. H. Levin and W. B. Scot, it is indicated that Lumpfish probably does not have scales. Prof. Carl Gans indicated to me that in a monograph on Lumpfish in 1911 (in German) by Albrecht Hase it is stated that the Lumpfish has scales but these are like the scales found on sharks rather than on teleosts. Hence, we would consider Lumpfish forbidden.

Mahi-Mahi was questioned because it was unclear whether it is in the porpoise or the dolphin family. The Marine Fisheries Service gives this information. Mahi-mahi is the Hawaiian common name of the dolphinfish *Coryphaena hippurus* which has fins and scales although the scales are very small. *Fishery Leaflet 531* of the Bureau lists it among the fish that have fins and scales. Hence we consider mahi-mahi as kosher.

QUESTION: *May vessels be koshered by means of autoclaving?*

ANSWER: Autoclaving is to kosher by means of steam rather than water. According to the *Shulhan Arukh,* only water can serve the purpose of kashering (O.H. 451:5). However, since the purpose of kashering is to rid the utensils of any of the forbidden substance they might have absorbed it is logical to infer that any process that will have this effect should be permitted. There is no question that in autoclaving the steam under pressure penetrates more than water and has a more potent effect, hence it should be permitted. See: *She'eilot u-Teshuvot Maharsham*, part 1, no. 94; *She'eilot u'Teshuvot Yad Yitzhak*, part 2, no. 267; *She'eilot u-Teshuvot Avnei Neizer*, Yoreh De'ah, part 1, no. 111; *Hagahot Maharsham*, O.H. 451:3; *Yad Meir*, No. 1; *She'eilot u-Teshuvot Maharam Shick, Tluta'i* no. 125.

QUESTION: *What is the status of Pyrex, Corningware and the variety of the new materials used in the manufacture of dishes?*

ANSWER: The problem involved in these questions is whether these are in the category of glass dishes, which may be used for milk and meat without kashering, or in the category of earthenware, which may not be kashered at all, or do they form a third category?

The reason earthenware may not be kashered is because *kli heres eino yotzei midei dofyo l'olam*, earthenware is so porous that no amount of kashering can purge it of what it has absorbed (B. Pesahim 30b) and also, *d'has aleihen dilma pakei*, for fears that the heat will cause them to crack (B. Pesahim 30b) and they will not be kashered properly. Glassware needs no kashering because it is hard and nonporous and smooth and therefore does not absorb. Furthermore, it is generally not used for hot liquids and therefore does not need kashering. (Oreh Hayim 451:26, and also in Bi'ur Hagra, ad loc.).

In the case of Pyrex and similar materials it would seem that because of their hardness and because they are nonporous they are in the same category as glassware. But unlike glassware, they are used for cooking and the concern that the heat will cause them to crack does not exist. Hence, the majority of the authorities maintain that we apply to these the rules we apply to metal utensils, i.e., that they may be kashered by boiling, but they may not be used for both milk and meat though they are hard and nonporous like glass. (See *Sha'erey Halakha*, Rabbi Shimon Efrati, v. 1., no. 2; *She'eilot u'Teshuvot Tzitz Eliezer*, Eliezer Yehudah Waldenberg, v. 9, no. 26: *She'arim Hamtzuyanim B'halakha*, v. 3., p. 108; *She'eilot u-Teshuvot Seridei Eish*, Harav Yehiel Ya'akov Weinberg, v. 2., no. 76, 160; *She'eilot u-Teshuvot Havalim Banimin*, Yehudah

Leib Graubart, v. 4, no. 56.) See, however, *She'eilot u-Teshuvot Yabia Omer*, Harav Ovadiah Yosef, v. 4, Y.D., no. 5 who permits Pyrex dishes to be used for milk and meat. This we would not recommend, just as we do not recommend having just one set of glass dishes to use for both milk and meat (See above, *teshuva* on glass dishes).

QUESTION: *May the circumcision of an adult be done with the patient under anesthesia?*

ANSWER: This question usually comes up in the case of an adult male convert. It comes up also with Jews who were not circumcised as infants either because their parents had refused, on principle, to have it done, and the sons when grown up are of a different mind, or because, in times of persecution as during the Nazi Holocaust many children were not circumcised because of the danger involved; or with the Jews coming out of Soviet Russia who did not circumcise their children because it would incur the "displeasure" of the powers that be.

The problems are that under anesthesia it is impossible to apply the principle of *mitzvot tzerikhot kavanah* ("the performance of a *mitzvah* needs conscious intent") ; and that the *mohel* has to be the *shaliah* ("appointed agent") of the person undergoing circumcision, and under anesthesia one is not able to make such an appointment.

The answer to these strictures is that it is the *mohel*, and not the patient, that needs *kavanah*, and that the appointment of the *shaliah* can be executed before the anesthesia is applied.

When local anesthesia is applied the above objections certainly do not apply (Rabbi Ovadiah Yosef in *Noam*, v. 12, pp 1-10 *She'eilot, u-Teshuvot Mimama'akim*, R. Efrayim Oshri v. 2, no. 15).

QUESTION: *Does one say* Yizkor *for a deceased relative during the first year after his death?*

ANSWER: The custom that prevails in many communities has been not to recite *Yizkor* before a year has elapsed since the death of the person. The explanation given is that during the first year the pain is still fresh and the recital of *Yizkor* will evoke excessive tears and sorrow and thus interfere with the joy of the festival (see *Ziv ha-Minhagim*, Rabbi J. D. Singer, p. 201).

This practice is not universal, however. Some authorities feel on the contrary, that the first year is the most appropriate time to recite it (*Shei'eilot u-Teshuvot Hillel Omeir*, Harav Hillel Posek, nos. 320, 305).

We would suggest that we adopt the practice of reciting *Yizkor* during the first year, too, especially since today many people who come to worship at the synagogue do so only on such occasions. Hence, there is the additional *mitzvah* of bringing these people to the synagogue to worship. *V'dai l'hakima* . . .

QUESTION : *May a person bequeath his eyes to be used after his death for the living who have lost their eyesight?*

ANSWER : This was the first item in the now wider general question of transplants. Since in this case the eye is transplanted only after the donor had definitely ceased to live, the following issues are involved :

   a. the question of *nivul ha-met*, the disfiguring of a dead body which is forbidden;
   b. the question of *met assur behana'ah*, that one may not derive any benefit from a dead body;
   c. that the remains of a person must be buried (*kevurah*).

Practically all the authorities permit bequeathing an eye. Some authorities, however, have the following reservations : the beneficiary must be totally blind; the donor must will his eye to a specific person rather than to an eye bank; and only the cornea may be removed rather than the whole eyeball.

The *heter* meets the objections that we mentioned above as follows : The objection on the ground of *nivul ha-met* is not valid here because when it helps a living person it is a *kavod ha-met*, an honor to the dead, rather than *nivul ha-met;* the objection that the dead body is *asur b'hana'ah* does not apply when it is used for medical purposes (*mitrapin b'issurei hana'ah*) ; as to the obligation of burial, since the eye is grafted on another living human being, it will eventually be buried even though it is transplanted. Furthermore, when transplanted, it becomes living tissue to which the obligation of burial does not apply.

In the case of an eye there is an additional reason to permit it. Rabbi Unterman takes the talmudic statement *suma hashuv k'meit* ("a blind person is accounted as a dead person") literally, and, therefore, the question of *pikuah nefesh* ("saving a life") is involved, and *pikuah nefesh* supersedes all other prohibitions. See: *Shevet m'Yehudah*, Iser Yehudah Unterman p. 313; Rabbi Simhah Halevy Levy, *Hadarom*, Elul 721, p. 31, Tishri 723. p. 191; *Kol Bo al Aveilut*, Yekuthiel Gruenwald, p. 45; Rabbi Theodor Friedman, *Rabbinical Assembly Proceedings*, 1953, p. 41 ff.; Rabbi Isaac Klein, Responsum on Autopsy, Conservative Judaism, Summer 1959. Rabbinical Council of America, Proceedings 1948, p. 50.

QUESTION: *If a burial took place during the Intermediate Days (Hol Ha-Mo'ed) when do the mourners cut Keriah?*

ANSWER: The prevailing practice, at least as far as I have learned, has been to wait with the *Keriah* until the conclusion of the Festival, to coincide with the beginning of mourning. And yet the *Shulhan Arukh* (*Yoreh De'ah* 340:31) forbids *Keriah* only during the Festival days, but requires it during the Intermediate Days. The Ramo (ibid.) mentions the *minhag* that for a father and a mother *Keriah* is cut during the Intermediate Days, but for other relatives one must wait until the conclusion of the Festival. Then the Ramo adds the ruling that where there is no established *minhag* one should cut *Keriah* during the Intermediate Days at all funerals that require it.

In spite of the general practice not to cut *Keriah* during the Intermediate Days there is now an increasing feeling that to wait with the *Keriah*—which actually should take place *b'sha'at himum*, when the pain is most acute—until after the Festival is an anticlimax which does not have the desired effect and defeats its purpose. Hence, we suggest that we cut *Keriah* during the Intermediate Days as on any other weekday, though we start the *Shivah* after the conclusion of the Festival.

16. AN APPROACH TO HALAKHA (1955)

I chose as title for this study "A Conservative Approach to Jewish Law." The title is worded that way advisedly because, at present, we only have a *conservative approach* to Jewish law. Some people would like to see the Conservative movement come forth with a ready-made *Shulhan Arukh* with a specific Conservative answer to everything. This cannot be done now first, because we are not yet ready for it; we are still too young and it takes time for a movement to become crystallized into concrete regulations. Secondly, we do not want to freeze the development of the movement at this point. It would be unhealthy to do so since the public is not receptive to any law at present. We must create a climate that is more receptive. Some practices have to take root first.

There are, however, certain lines of development that we can recognize, and it is these that we would like to discuss, but we must first state some basic assumptions that I subscribe to:

1. We believe in Torah *min hashamayim*, that our laws are divinely inspired.
2. We affirm that Halakha is normative and has a central role in Jewish life.
3. We affirm that the law has not been frozen but can grow to meet new situations.

The first assumption is that we believe in Torah *min hashamayim*, we believe the Torah is divine. A religious law is not in the same class as a law promulgated by a legislature. According to some, when the prophets and lawgivers of Israel spoke, it was not as today, when a judge speaks from the bench. There are amongst us those who would say that this is exactly what they are. The humanists among us would interpret the religious odyssey of our people in terms of cause and effect. We disagree with them.

We also disagree with those who take *Torah m'Sinai* literally and

128

who would say that God lectured to Moses the way a lecturer addresses his audience, Moses took notes as it were and that each word of the Bible was thus literally spoken by God.

We believe that the law is a cooperative product of the human and the divine. Man was in search of God but God was also in search of man. The law is the response of man to God's admonition. The words of the Torah then became like a seed that grows into a mighty plant.

We also affffirm the central and normative role of Halakhah in Judaism. Judaism has many strands. In the Talmud we have the *Halakhah and the Aggadah.* Halakhah is normative law that prescribes our conduct; Aggadah appeals to our emotions and our imagination. It is the poetry of our religion while the Halakhah is the prose. It fires our imagination and inspires our thoughts. There is the *simhah shel mitzvah,* the joy that comes from performing a *mitzvah.* There is the outpouring of prayer that breaks through the framework of rules and regulations. There is the mystical experience that is unaware of any limits. There are the songs of praise that burst forth beyond any prescribed boundaries. There is piety that sees in rules unnecessary fetters that hamper the spirit.

All these make the mosaic of our faith and give it a wide range of appeal. *And yet, we insist that Halakhah is the core, it is central.* To use a term in our educational system, the others are elective subjects while Halakhah is a prescribed subject; it is a must. It is *Halakha* that is the main character of Judaism that gave it its present day form.

We also affirm that the law has not been frozen, but can grow to meet new situations. There is an old controversy between jurists whether law is an open or a closed system. Closed means complete with provisions for every possibility and contingency. Open where it is recognized that the law is incomplete and must be revised periodically with new provisions added. The argument against considering law a closed system is that no actual set of rules devised by any human agency can possibly foresee all contingencies and provide for them; hence, the judge who has to decide all the cases that come before him must necessarily legislate and thus fill the gaps of incompleteness in existing law.

Professor Morris Raphael Cohen defends the closed system

against this stricture by distinguishing between formal and material completeness. Let us take science as an analogy. In natural science, although the system is constantly changing through the assimilation of new information, it is still complete, because all the changes are made with the principle immanent in science. *It is complete because it is self-corrective.*

Similarly, any legal system, such as that of the American Constitution, can be said to be complete if legislation or amendment to it is made in accordance with its own provisions.

Halakhah is in this category. The psalmist says *Torat adonai temimah,* the law of God is perfect, it is complete because it is self-corrective. Within Jewish law itself are principles that help it to grow and adjust.

It is these principles that formed the progressive character of the Halakhah. The Conservative approach has stressed that history and sociology enter into the formation of the Halakhah. While it was divine in origin, the human element inevitably entered into it. In the Talmud, this is expressed in the form of the following story:

Rabbi Joshua and Rabbi Eleazer were arguing about a point of law. To prove his point, Rabbi Eleazer invoked divine witnesses. He invited a voice from Heaven to proclaim the validity of his opinion. To this, Rabbi Joshua gave the famous retort: *Lo bashamayim hi*—"The Torah is not in Heaven"; God gave the Torah to us and now we have to validate our opinions by human means.

Anyone acquainted with the history of Jewish law cannot help but realize that this has been a fact. Of course, human conditions enter into the growth of the law. It is only in recent generations that the law was frozen and made into an absolute.

Thus, for instance, in the introduction to his book *Agan Hasahar,* Rabbi Hayim Zimmerman gives classic expression to this view. In his book he discusses the question of the international date line. One authority, Rabbi Menahem Kasher, has maintained that, fortunately, the line is drawn in the Pacific Ocean where there are no inhabitants thus preventing the confusion that might have resulted if there were two cities, one on one side of the line and the other on the other side of the line; one keeping Shabbat on one day, and the other keeping it another day. Rabbi Zimmerman sternly rebukes such considerations. Wherever the line is drawn, that is where it has to be and human considerations may not enter into it. Historically, such a view is not valid. Let me give you one example of the development of law among our strict Orthodox brethren, which proves my point.

The question of the permissibility of autopsy according to Jewish law comes up very frequently. Today, we understand the problem very well. We have Jewish hospitals and Jewish doctors who are very much interested in the problem.

The first recorded instance of the question in the form of a formal legal decision comes to us from the famous eighteenth-century rabbi of Prague, Ezekiel Landau. Surgery was performed on a man who suffered from gallstones in the city of London, and he died. The doctors wanted permission for an autopsy in order to improve their techniques for future cases.

Rabbi Landau answered that the only case where autopsy is permissible is where there is a possibility of saving a life thereby. According to Rabbi Landau, this means that there is another person before us sick with the same ailment, and that through an autopsy on the dead patient we might help the living.

Two hundred years later, the rabbis permitted autopsies in any case where something new might be learned or the doctor's skill in treatment of the disease could be improved, provided all the organs dissected would be treated with the proper reverence. This would also include the use of cadavers in medical schools. This version of the law is included in the agreement between the Hadassah Medical School and the chief rabbinate.

What has happened between the days of Rabbi Landau and the present-day rabbinate in Israel? Is it that today's rabbis are greater scholars than Rabbi Landau? I doubt it. Is it that they are more liberal? That is not true, either.

The only answer is that there are certain sociologic forces that operate today that did not operate in the days of Rabbi Landau. First of all, the science of medicine has grown and the need for autopsies grew with it. Furthermore, there was the pressure of medical schools that needed bodies for dissection and the urging of physicians who had special cases. In a number of European medical schools it became an issue upon which depended whether or not Jewish candidates would be accepted in medical schools.

These conditions, to put it mildly, have influenced a revision in rabbinic decisions. The law has grown as a result of sociologic conditions.

There are many instances of this sort in the past. In talmudic times, the law was certainly such that conditions led the rabbis to modify it. There is the famouse case of the *prosbol*. I am sure many of you have heard about it. Let me just refresh your memory.

According to biblical law, all debts are canceled every Sabbatical year. In a simple agricultural economy this does not cause too much difficulty. Loans are mostly short-term. The farmer borrows money in the spring for seed; at harvesttime, he pays it back. If he has not paid it back by the Sabbatical year, his must be a case of hardship and the debt should therefore be canceled.

Later on, when the simple agricultural economy gave way to a commercial economy, this proved impractical. How can you conduct business without long-term credits? A way had to be found to adjust the law so as not to interfere with business. To abrogate the law was out of the question; biblical laws could not be abrogated. Hillel enacted a *takkanah* that circumvented this difficulty. Theoretically, of course, the arrival of the Sabbatical year still canceled all debts. Hillel arranged, however, that all debts be registered in court. This registration made the debt as good as collected.

A more recent example has to do with the problem of a wife whose husband suffered shipwreck or was drowned. May she remarry? Of course she may remarry, you will say; she is a widow. It is not as simple as that. You must be sure that the person is dead. Suppose we did not recover his body? We may have seen him drown, but he may have reappeared somewhere else.

The rabbis of the Talmud have, therefore, made a distinction between *mayyim she'ein lo'hem sof,* water that has no end, i.e., whose shore we cannot see and *mayyim sh'yesh lo'hem sof,* waters that have a boundary, i.e., whose shore you can see. If you see a man drown in a lake, even if the body is not recovered we consider him dead because if he should reappear on another shore, we would see him. On the other hand, if he should drown in the ocean, it is quite possible that he could emerge from the waters where we could not see him. Hence, we cannot be sure he is dead.

During the nineteenth century when the great wave of immigration started, this became an acute problem. Many people were lost on the sea voyage and their wives remained *agunot*, that is, they could not remarry.

The problem was brought before Rabbi Isaac Elhanan, the great rabbi of Kovno, and he declared that in our day all bodies of water are accounted as *mayyim sh'yesh lo'hem sof*, as waters that have a boundary. Today, there is no longer unexplored territory to which the person may go. With modern means of communication, a person can inform us of his whereabouts no matter where he is. If, therefore, there are witnesses that have seen him drown, it is sufficient (*Ayin Yitzhak* 22:3:20; *Be'er Yitzhak*, E. H. 18: See also *Hatam Sofer* E. H. 58, 65).

Thus, there is no question that the Halakhah was always flexible and always reacted to the sociologic changes. We would say that the law was always in history, never outside of it. Now, whereas I surmise that our Orthodox brethren may have reacted in most cases unconsciously to the pressure of the environment, we do it consciously and intentionally. We are thus much more in the tradition than those who would freeze the law.

The best example is what the conservative rabbinate has done with the *ketubah*. In biblical and talmudic times, the power to divorce rested with the husband only. Do not get any idea that he had a free hand. The *ketubah* protected the woman by making the divorce an expensive affair. It prescribed the obligations of the husband and the rights of the wife.

During the tenth century, the famous Rabbenu Gershon of Mainz, heading a synod of rabbis, issued a ban against polygamy and decreed as well that henceforth the formal consent of the woman was also necessary in case of a divorce. When the Jewish courts had power, they had no difficulty convincing either party to consent when it felt justified in issuing a divorce. In Israel, where the rabbinic courts have this power today, the Jewish divorce laws operate very smoothly. The difficulty arises in a country like America, where the rabbinic courts have no powers of coercion. If one of the parties refuses to cooperate, we are in real trouble. For people who abide by the law, this often results in suffering and tragedy. If it is the woman who refuses her consent to a divorce, there are ways of overcoming it. If it is the man who refuses to give the divorce, there is nothing that we can do about it. Evidently, the law in this case is unfair to the woman and favors the man. The

Conservative rabbinate has added a paragraph to the *ketubah* which eliminated this advantage in favor of the husband. It states that if either the husband or the wife demands a divorce, both must appear before a rabbinic court and abide by its decision and affix their signature to it. If one refuses, the other party can sue for breach of contract.

This is one example of how the law grows and meets new situations.

Now you may ask: Why are roundabout ways necessary? Why not just legislate that from now on the law is changed and if the husband refuses to give a *get* the rabbi, when he feels it is justified, should issue it without the consent of the husband. Or why not do what our reform brethren do? They say we do not need a *get* at all.

The second alternative is not acceptable because it is like telling a patient to get rid of a headache by cutting off his head. The headache is certainly eliminated, but together with too much else.

To the first question, we have the following answer. Roscoe Pound, the great American jurist and dean of the Harvard Law School said: "Law must be stable, and yet it cannot stand still." (*Interpretation of Legal History*, p. 1) Justice Cardozo, in his little classic, *The Growth of the Law*, says that one of the great needs of American law was "a philosophy that will mediate between the conflicting claims of stability and progress, and supply a principle of growth" (p. 1).

For a law to operate, it must have stability. That gives it its authority. When a law changes too frequently and too radically, you have a lot of progress but no stability. On the other hand, if you stand pat, there may be stability but there is no progress and the result is stagnation. We therefore must have both. Hence, our insistence upon making the changes in the manner we described. Formally, we retain the integrity of the law and, at the same time, make room for progress. This formula satisfies both needs of the law and helps to make it operative.

Of course, the big problem is how to make our people respect the authority of the law and abide by it.

17. THE SHULHAN ARUKH AFTER 400 YEARS (1968)

In the year 1567 (5357) a book was printed in Venice with this legend on its title page:

> *The Shulhan Arukh*
>
> authorized by his eminence, the marvel of the generation, the perfect sage, our master, Rabbi Joseph Karo, may the Merciful protect him and keep him healthy, the son of Ephrayim Karo, for his instruction is brief and pure, in the month of Sivan, 5327 Anno Mundi, here in Venice, the Metropolis. Juan Grifi, the printer.

At the end of the book appears this legend: "And the completion of this precious book took place Sunday night, the 28th of Nisan, the year 327 according to the minor reckoning. Perfected and completed."

Last year was thus the 400th anniversary of the *Shulhan Arukh* of Rabbi Joseph Karo about which it was said: "There is no other book in Israel, after the Talmud, worthy of achieving such wide acceptance by the people as the *Shulhan Arukh,* and there is no other book that deserved to have so many commentators, who carefully study its words, almost its letters, as was done with the Scroll of the Torah (Rav Tsa'ir, *Toldot ha-Posekim,* v. 3, p. 1).

The Jewish world has taken cognizance of this fact, and we of the Rabbinical Assembly wish to join in paying our tribute to one of the towering figures in our history whose influence on Jewish life has been all-pervasive and is still a great factor in our lives today.

It was the sixteenth century. For the Jews it was the period after the expulsion from Spain, which was called the third *hurban.* It resulted not only in a great deal of physical suffering, but also in the dislocation of large numbers of people, the demise of eminent Jewish communities which had enjoyed a long and distinguished history, the rise of new ones that were about to make their own

135

mark, and the vitalization and revival of many existent communities. There was a yearning for a Zion rebuilt and for some tangible efforts to reconstruct its ruins.

In the world at large, or the outside world that the Jews knew, there was ferment and upheaval. It was the period of the Reformation and the resultant fratricidal wars. It was also the century of great explorations following upon Columbus's voyages and the discovery of America.

It was also marked by the rise and the decline of empires.

Most of the Jews who had escaped from Spain eventually landed in Islamic countries, particularly in the hospitable Ottoman Empire which was then at the peak of its power. Among the refugees who found a haven there was the family of Rabbi Joseph Karo, the author of the *Shulhan Arukh*. It was a distinguished family from Toledo in Spain and counted a number of scholars on its family tree. Joseph Karo was born in Toledo in 1488. In 1492, when he was four years old, his family joined the thousands of its brethren who left Spain because of the expulsion, and settled in Portugal. With the expulsion from Portugal which soon followed, the Karo family experienced a period of weary and painful wandering, and settled in Nicopolis, a city in what is today northern Bulgaria. Their stay was temporary, for in a few years (C 1518) we find the family in the Greek city of Adrianople, from which they went on to Salonika and Constantinople. By 1535, Karo had settled in Palestine.

It was in Adrianople in the year 1522 (5282), that Karo started his magnum opus, *Bet Yosef,* a commentary on Jacob ben Asher's *Arba'ah Turim*. He worked on it for twenty years, and then for twelve more years, checking and revising. When the work was completed he was already in Safed, whither he came in the year 1536 (5296) and where he lived for the rest of his life.

While Karo is known better today for his later work, the *Shulhan Arukh* ("Prepared Table"), 1564–1565, it is his *Bet Yosef* that is the greater work and that, according to Professor Louis Ginzberg, marks him as one of the greatest Talmudists of all times (*Jewish Encyclopedia,* vol. 3, p. 585). Yet, it was through his later work— of lesser stature and practically merely an abbreviation of his greater work giving just a bare conclusion in succinct legal statements—that his greater influence was felt.

As is well known, the code was greeted with sharp opposition by

Ashkenazi scholars who complained of its bias in favor of the Sephardi practice. It was soon supplemented by Rabbi Moses Isserles (RAMO) who presented the practice as well as the opinions of the Ashkenazi Jewish community, thus making it acceptable to both Ashkenazim and Sephardim. Eventually, it became the authoritative norm accepted by *klal yisroel,* so that one authority proclaimed: "He who opposes him is as if he would oppose the Shekhina" (*She'eilot u-Teshuvot ha-Ramo,* responsa 48).

What was the purpose of Karo's work and why did it achieve such wide acceptance and influence?

Rabbi Joseph Karo himself provides the answer. In his introduction he tells us that what prompted him to devote his life to his work was that he saw a need to review all practical laws of Judaism, explaining their sources in the Talmud, and all the conflicting interpretations concerning them, because the situation of the time was liable to divide the Torah, not merely into two Torahs, but numberless Torahs (see, Introduction, *Orah Hayim*). This threat was very real because of the unstable situation brought about by the great dislocation of the Jewish population.

The new situation, similar to our own in many respects, brought up new questions. No other period, except perhaps the one we live in, was so rich in responsa literature. The new life of these exiles created new problems that pressed for answers. And the answers were forthcoming in abundance. In spite of the unfavorable conditions under which the exiles struggled for bare survival, the time was rich in great scholars. Because there were so many scholars, each one of them relegated to himself the prerogative of being a *Posek Aharon* (Rav Tsa'ir, *Toldot ha-Posekim,* vol. 3, p. 12). There was a clear need for a work that would clarify these differences, study them critically, and arrive at a single conclusion. To be sure, this required great scholarship as well as an author who would command the respect of his peers. Many felt the need for such a work, but it was the *zekhut* of Rabbi Joseph Karo to do it. He was eminently suited for the task by scholarship, by his perseverence, and by his genuine humility and piety.

He chose the code of another scholar around which to write his work rather than write a separate and independent work finding this method eminently suitable for his purpose. Karo's intention was to present each law, discuss it, and arrive at a conclusion regarding it. Furthermore, he wanted to avoid duplication, or at least to reduce it to a minimum.

There were two such preeminent codes available for his choice, the *Mishneh Torah* of Maimonides, and the *Tur* of Rabbi Jacob ben Asher (c. 1280–1340). Several reasons induced Karo to write his work around the *Tur* rather than around the code of Maimonides, which was far more famous and widespread. First, the *Tur*, although not considered as great an authority as the Rambam, was the most popular textbook of its time and hence more familiar to the people (Isidore Twersky, *Judaism*, Spring 1967, p. 143, note 9). Maimonides' code was recognized mainly among the Spanish Jews, while the *Tur* enjoyed a high reputation among the Ashkenazim and the Sefardim as well as among the Italian Jews (*Jewish Encyclopedia*, v. 3, p. 585).

Second, it was not Karo's intention to create a code similar in form to Maimonides' code. He intended to give, not merely the result of his investigations, but also the investigations themselves; thus not only aiding the officiating rabbi in the performance of his duties of rendering decisions, but also tracing the development of particular laws from the Talmud through later rabbinic literature for the student. The study of talmudic literature was for Karo, not a means to an end, i.e., merely a guide for religious observance, but an end in itself. He, therefore, did not favor codes that contained only final decisions, without giving the reasons for these decisions and how they were arrived at (ibid.). It also should be remembered that the *Tur* was a later work and it, therefore, contained material not found in Maimonides and omitted material contained in Maimonides but not relevant to the times (see R. Yekuthiel Grunwald, *Harav Yossef Karo Uzmano*, p. 158, n. 6). Thus, generally speaking, the *Tur* was more suitable for his purpose since Maimonides was too concise and monolithic, presenting, on the whole, unilateral, undocumented decisions. The *Tur* was expansive and more interpretive, citing alternate views and presenting divergent explanations (Twersky, p. 143).

Actually the *Bet Yosef* was an independent work, not just a commentary. Karo would first explain each law in the text of the *Tur* and discuss whether the rule in the text was a result of consensus or was subject to dispute. He also explained the alternate interpretation that the *Tur* presented and rejected. He sometimes also adds and explains those views which the *Tur* omitted. Then he would give his own normative ruling. He thus accomplished two purposes. He explained the text, filled it with flesh and blood, and then added his own legal decision.

Karo wrote the *Shulhan Arukh* in his old age. He wrote it as a review or a synopsis of his major work for the benefit of those who did not possess the education necessary to understand his *Bet Yosef*. Thus the author himself held no very high opinion of his work, saying that he had written it chiefly for *talmidim k'tanim* and never refers in his responsa to the *Shulhan Arukh* but rather to the *Bet Yosef*.

The *Shulhan Arukh* achieved its popularity, not only against the wishes and expectations of the author, but, curiously enough, through the very scholars who attacked it (*Jewish Encyclopedia*, vol. 3, p. 585 f.). It was attacked severely even by his Sefardi contemporaries such as Rabbi Yom-Tob Zahalon, Rabbi Jacob Castro, Rabbi Samuel Abuhab, and others. They called it a book for children and for the laity. It was even whispered that it was the work of some of his students who were instructed to write an abstract of the *Bet Yosef* (*Devar Shmuel*, sec. 255). Others suggested patronizingly that it was a child of his old age and that he could not give this work the necessary care and attention because he was ill (see, *Encyclopedia Judaica*, ix, p. 1001).

It was even more vehemently challenged by the Ashkenazi scholars of Poland which was now becoming the greatest center of Jewish learning. The two great luminaries in the large galaxy of scholars of the period were the Ramo, from Cracow, in Poland (1520–1573) and the Maharshal, from Lublin (1510–1573). Both strongly criticised Karo's work. Rabbi Moses Isserles protested that the *Bet Yosef* mentioned only Spanish and ignored the Franco-German and Polish authorities. He further objected to Karo's complete neglect of the place of *minhag* in Jewish law which Isserles considered of great importance and not to be omitted in a code. Shlomo ben Yehiel Luria, also an Ashkenazi, shared the Ramo's great respect for the Franco-German scholars whom he placed above the Sephardic, and added that since the completion of the Talmudim, or the halakhic midrashim, no opinion that cannot be deduced from them could claim to be authoritative (*Jewish Encyclopedia*, III, p. 586).

The greatest challenge came from a disciple of Isserles and Luria,

Rabbi Mordecai Yaffe, the author of the *Levush*. He had the same objections as his teacher to both the *Bet Yosef* and the *Shulhan Arukh*. He had originally started to prepare a guide in the manner of the *Bet Yosef,* but when the *Bet Yosef* appeared, he realized that his work would be superfluous. He then wished to write a book that would summarize the *Bet Yosef* and add reasons and explanations for each law. Because of the expulsion of the Jewish community from Moravia, where he lived, the work was delayed. News then reached him that the *Shulhan Arukh* of Karo was about to appear, and again he was disappointed, believing that he would have nothing new to offer. However, when the *Shulhan Arukh* made its appearance, he found it inadequate and thought he would supplement it. He then learned that his teacher, Isserles, had done just that and he came to the conclusion that there was no room for the type of work that he had in mind. He decided that he should carry out his original intention. The result was the *Levush*. In his introduction, the author tells us that he made his work neither as long as the *Bet Yosef* nor as short as the *Shulhan Arukh*. He managed to incorporate what he felt Karo had omitted, addressing himself mainly to the problems that great halakhists, ethicists, philosophers, and mystics have constantly confronted: how to maintain a rigid, punctilious observance of the law and, concomitantly, avoid externalization and routinization (Twersky, p. 155).

For a while it seemed that the *Levush* was a worthy contestant to take the place of the *Shulhan Arukh,* and almost succeeded in doing so. It was a pupil of Isserles, Rabbi Yehoshua Falk, one of the first and greatest commentators on the *Shulhan Arukh,* who was responsible for the predominance of the *Shulhan Arukh*. In his commentary (*Sefer Meirat Einayim*) he constantly refuted the position of the *Levush* and thus undermined his authority.

Where did the strength of the *Shulhan Arukh* lie? There is no question but that the supplement of Isserles and the many commentaries helped make the code so widely accepted. That, however, was a result and not the cause of its prevailing acceptance. It is suggested that the very quality that aroused so much criticism was the reason for its popularity: its tone of authority, the short decision given without explanation or source. The age was ready for just such a type of code. The work appealed to lay people as well as to scholars. There is no doubt that the supplement of Isserles

was largely responsible for making the *Shulhan Arukh* acceptable
to the Ashkenazi community of Eastern Europe which was even
then the *rov minyan v'rov binyan* of *k'lal Yisroel*. He was followed
by the well-known commentators who helped in this process of
establishing the *Shulhan Arukh* as the code and particularly as
final authority (*She'eilot u-Teshuvot Ha Ramo*, responsum 48).
They acted both as cause and effect; effect because the scholars felt
that since the *Shulhan Arukh* was so popular it must be brought up
to date, and because they brought it up to date its popularity and
authority became more firmly established.

All this leads us to our major question: Can the *Shulhan Arukh*
still serve as the authoritative code today? Is it still relevant?

If Karo found that, in his day, because of the chaotic situation
resulting from the upheavals in the world and in the Jewish community, a new code was necessary, what would he have thought
had he lived today? To be sure, as we have mentioned, our time
is similar in some ways to the turbulent era that Karo lived in;
but it is also radically different, with utterly different social conditions, a totally different intellectual climate, and completely different needs and demands. One major and basic difference is that
whereas the author of the *Shulhan Arukh* and his commentators
labored in the midst of a people imbued with an intense spirit of
piety and saintliness among whom the saint was the hero, we live
in a time when the Zeitgest is hostile to piety and saintliness, and
the climate of opinion is that of sophisticated skepticism. It was a
pious age, not only in comparison with our generation, but also
compared to the ages that preceded it. Hence, whereas the code of
Maimonides begins with a philosophic dissertation giving a rational
basis for religion, the *Shulhan Arukh* begins by exhorting the Jew
to be cognizant at all times of the presence of God and to motivate
his conduct by this belief. Our age is closer to the age of Maimonides
than to the age of Karo.

Much has happened since Karo and Isserles, particularly among
the most recent generations. The results are well known: A large
segment of the Jewish community has defected; another segment
espouses a secularist philosophy of Judaism; still another group
remains within the religious orbit, but considers Halakhah irrelevant. With reluctance we confess that even within the orbit of the
devotees of Halakhah there is unrest and much straining at the

leash. In addition, many, while superficially professing adherence to Halakhah, honor it more in the breach than in the observance.

It is proper to mention that Karo faced some of the difficulties that every codifier confronts. In our discussion, we omitted the *maggid,* that mysterious oracle that played such a large role in the life and work of Joseph Karo, because it would have taken us too far afield from our major purpose. It is relevant, however, to relate that the sayings of the *maggid* reflect the conflicts and fears that Karo faced in writing his code. He was uncomfortable about making decisions on questions about which the authorities he followed held conflicting opinions. His generation saw the rise of mysticism and its influence on Jewish life and practice; Karo, too, was greatly influenced by it. He, therefore, sometimes had to make decisions between the teachings of *Nigleh,* the standard halakhic works, and *Nistar,* the mystical teachings that were at times in conflict with it (*Toldot ha-Posekim* v. 3, p. 20).

In our day a codifier would face such difficulties and conflicts in a different way. Today, conflicts have arisen because of new social conditions, the emancipation of women, new economic conditions, the rise of technology, electronics, and automation, and the advances in medical science. There is also an ethical sensitivity that views some of the laws as harsh. With all that, our conclusion is that the *Shulhan Arukh* is still a valid guide. Let me qualify this with a quotation from a paper read at the 1939 Rabbinical Assembly convention almost thirty years ago. At this convention, Dr. Boaz Cohen said, "The purpose of the various codes was utilitarian and not authoritarian, namely: 1. the systemization of the large body of rules in order to facilitate access to the findings of the law; 2. the determination of the law in case of conflicting opinions; 3. the incorporation of new decisions and customs that accumulated in the course of time."

Consequently, in accordance with their historical conception, the *Shulhan Arukh* has no more claim to our unquestioned obedience than the *Mishneh Torah* or the *Semag* or the *Tur,* yet we should accept the *Shulhan Arukh* as a guide for religious practice which was all that Karo intended it to be (*Cohen, Law and Tradition,* p. 70).

This we should supplement with a later statement by another contemporary scholar. He said: "The *Shulhan Arukh* is not a revealed canon, nor is it a hypostasis of the law. In the long creative history of the Oral Law it is one more link connecting Rav Hai Gaon, Maimonides, Nahmanides, Rabbi Salamon ibn Adret with Rabbi Elijah Gaon of Vilna, Rabbi Akiba Eiger, and Rabbi Joseph Rosen. It is a significant work which, for a variety of reasons, became a repository and a stimulus, a treasure and inspiration for Halakhah, both practice and study" (Isidore Twersky, p. 142).

It is in this perspective that we hold the *Shulhan Arukh* in high esteem, especially since it is the last of the great codes, and the last that was accepted by *k'lal Yisroel*. And even this great code was accepted with qualifications and reservations. Beginning with Isserles and ending with the *Mishnah Berurah*, the *Shulhan Arukh* was qualified, modified, extended, limited, and interpreted to make room for new developments. We must remember that Isserles not only supplemented Karo, but also applied a different philosophy of law; he not only adapted the Ashkenazic practice to the Sephardic, but also insisted on the recognition of later authorities and on the emphasis of *minhag*. Whereas Karo followed the opinions of Alfasi, Maimonides, and Asheri and, when they differed, followed the majority opinion, Isserles followed the later Ashkenazi authorities and established the principle of *halakhah k'vatrai*—"the later authorities are the law" (see Isidore Twersky, p. 147).

This method, as well as the emphasis on *minhag*, would preserve established precedent and respect local custom, but it would also give recognition to later authorities, a very significant factor in the development of Halakhah. The commentators, too, did not just follow the *Shulhan Arukh* blindly; they tested each law against other opinions. Beginning with the Gaon of Vilna, there was further emphasis on talmudic sources as the final authority (see *Toldot ha-Posekim*, v. 3, p. 208).

The *Shulhan Arukh* served both as a stopping point and as a rallying point. In the past, they came at fairly regular intervals: The *Mishneh Torah* was published in the twelfth century, the *Tur* in the fourteenth century, and the *Shulhan Arukh* in the sixteenth century. Apparently the appearance of a new code is long overdue. Why has it not been written?

To be sure, some valiant efforts have been made. The most noteworthy example is the *Arukh Hashulhan*, which covers the entire area of the law as the *Shulhan Arukh* does. Others that gained wide circulation, but covered only part of the ground, are *Hayye Adam* and *Hokhmat Adam* of Rabbi Abraham Danzig, and *Mishnah Berurah* of the *Hofetz Hayim,* which is just a commentary on the *Orah Hayyim.* These, while very helpful, actually reveal one of the great obstacles that we face in these endeavors. Professor Schechter aptly remarked in another context, "The only mistake, perhaps, was that the successors of these *hassidim,* or pious men, of Germany regarded many of the religious customs that were merely the voluntary expression of particularly devout souls as worthy of imitation by the whole community, and made them obligatory upon all" (Schechter, *Studies in Judaism,* I, p. 210 f.).

The other obstacle is due to the petrification of Halakhah in the last few centuries which was, perhaps, a reaction to the new winds of doctrine that made themselves felt in the Jewish community. It was this age that proclaimed *hadash asur min haTorah,* and acted upon it. The guardians of Halakhah adopted this as their motto and put Halakhah into deep freeze. To use Dr. Schechter's description, "It is indeed a reign of authority, modified by accident" (*Studies in Judaism,* I, p. 210). If there was any reaction to the changed conditions it came unconsciously, *b'hesah hada'at* and by accident. The policy was to leave everything as it was.

We certainly cannot operate on these terms. Those of us who have a Conservative approach to Halakhah must be guided by other norms. First of all, we must reaffirm the fundamental principle that it is our aim to preserve the continuity of Jewish tradition which was maintained in unbroken succession from antiquity to our own day (See Professor Boaz Cohen, *Law and Tradition,* p. 89).

We must emphasize again and again that Halakhah is normative, the great vehicle of religious life. We must remember—especially those of us who sometimes feel like rebelling against the burden of the law, declaring it irrelevant—that "Law is dry and its details and burdensome only if its observance lacks vital commitment, but if all actions of a person are infused with the radical awareness that he is acting in the presence of God, then every detail becomes meaningful and relevant. Such an awareness rules out routine mechanical action; everything must be conscious and purposive in a God-oriented universe, where every step of man is directed towards God" (Twersky, p. 157).

We therefore cannot but recognize the *Shulhan Arukh* as the last great code accepted by *k'lal Yisroel*, which must therefore serve as our base of operation because there is no other. We have not repudiated it and I pray that we shall not. We shall, however, be guided by Dr. Schechter who said, "But however great the literary value of a code may be it does not invest it with the attribute of infallibility, nor does it exempt the student or the rabbi who makes use of it from the duty of examining each paragraph on its own merits, and subjecting it to the same rules of interpretation that were always applied to tradition" (Solomon Schechter, Studies in Judaism, I, p. 211).

We thus accept the *Shulhan Arukh* as a guide, but reserve the right to examine each rule and apply to it the "rules of interpretation that were always applied to tradition." Using these, we shall not operate in a vacuum but always take into consideration the sociological and historical factors that operate in our day. We are convinced that in the past, too, these factors operated and influenced the development of Halakhah. In our sophisticated age we shall want to proceed consciously, deliberately, and I pray with the awareness of the great sense of responsibility that it requires. We shall be guided by the needs of the community as well as by the desire to preserve and strengthen Halakhah as the guide to our lives.

Since it is hardly conceivable that a new code may arise that will be acceptable at present to *k'lal Yisroel*, we must think in terms of the philosophy that guided our movement and do what Isserles did in his day. He insisted on the authority of the scholars of Eastern Europe, and on the validity of the practices of these communities even if they did not agree with the law laid down by Rabbi Joseph Karo. That did not make the Sefardi Jews accept the decisions of Rabbi Moses Isserles. As we know, they continue to this day to follow Karo.

We, too, should insist on the authority of our scholars and on the validity of the practices in our congregations. As Isserles insisted on following the *aharonim* on the principle of *halakhah k'batrai*, we too should insist that our *aharonim* are within the tradition of the development of Halakhah and, like Isserles, are taking into consideration the now prevailing conditions and the new factors that operate in our time.

In this manner we shall do what the scholars of the past have done, bring the *Shulhan Arukh* up to date. However, there is a need that is becoming more and more apparent, that of doing what Karo and the other codifiers did rather than what Isserles did. We shall have to do it at least for the Conservative movement, and hope that it will be helpful to *k'lal Yisroel*. The obstacles are staggering, but the need is here.

One of our rabbinic scholars said: "The rabbinic system of law is based upon transcendental revelation interpreted and applied as best it may by the leading authorities of each generation disciplined for the task of a lifetime of scholarship and saintliness and informed by a deep sense of humility and responsibility" (Aaron Kirschenbaum, *Judaism*, Summer 1966, p. 364 ff.).

This prescription limits us a great deal. And yet we would add another requirement: a deep awareness of, and sympathy for the needs of the Jewish community. We pray that there be in our midst men who answer these requirements. They shall be the ones to write the code. All we can do is pray that men will develop in our movement qualified to do for us what Rabbi Joseph Karo and Rabbi Moses Isserles did for their generation.

18. BUSINESS ETHICS IN THE TALMUD (1949)

During the biblical era the children of Israel were almost entirely an agricultural people. Commerce was rare. The little that there was, was carried on by caravans of foreigners passing through the land; hence, the merchant was called a Canaanite. What little buying and selling was done was regulated by such commandments as; "Just balances, just weights, a just *ephah*, and a just *hin* shall you have" (Leviticus 19:36), and "Thou shalt not have in thy bag diverse weights, a great and a small. Thou shalt not have in thy house diverse measures, a great and a small. A perfect and just weight shalt thou have; a perfect and just measure shalt thou have; that thy days may be long upon the land which the Lord thy God giveth thee. For all that do such things, even all that do unrighteously, are an abomination unto the Lord thy God." (Deuteronomy 25:13–15).

In talmudic times commerce was already well developed and widespread among the Jews. It is no wonder, therefore, that a substantial part of the legal material in the Talmud is devoted to regulations governing business practices. The subject loomed so large that our sages suggested that when a person will appear for judgment before the heavenly court, the first question he will be asked will be: "Have you been honest in business" (B. Shabbat 19a)?

That the laws regulating business practices were not merely legal measures but also ethical deeds enjoined by religion is indicated in the Talmud when it says: "He who wants to live a pious life let him perform the things discussed in Nezekin" (B. Baba Kama 30a). Nezikin is the section of the Talmud that discusses matters that would come under the term "law" today. Evidently the maxim, "Business is business," was not countenanced. Rather was business considered as one means of pursuing a pious way of life by being ethical in its practice.

It is no wonder, therefore, that the Talmud has devoted so much space to the ethical conduct of business. The material we refer to

147

does not consist of utterances of saints speaking in pious language about ideal utopias, but of legal *dicta* by authorities setting standards for actual business practices. There is, of course, a graduation in the binding character of these dicta. Some are merely hortatory, where performance is recommended as a meritorious act for those who strive for high standards. These are in the categories of *middat hasidut,* the way of the pious, and *lifnim mishurat ha-din,* "beyond the requirement of the law." A category akin to it contains regulations where deviation is not punishable by law but is considered repugnant in the eyes of respectable citizens. Under these would also come practices termed *patur be-dineh adam v'hayav be-dineh shamayim,* "he is acquitted as far as human laws are concerned but is guilty in the eyes of the divine law." Most regulations, however, are normative in character and deviation from them is accounted a violation the remedy for which is enforceable by the courts.

Law and Ethics

Jurists have long argued about the difference between law and justice, and law and ethics, whether they are identical or have any relationship at all to each other. We shall ignore those who claim that law has nothing to do with justice and ethics, as those who espouse the imperative theory of law, for instance, because such theories will find no support in the Talmud. Taking Salmond's definition of law as "consisting of the rules in accordance with which justice is administered by judicial tribunes of the state" (Salmond, *Jurisprudence,* p. 49), the difference between law and ethics would depend upon the enforceability of a prescription. Ethical conduct is autonomous and must be completely voluntary without any outside coercion. Law, on the other hand, is heteronomous and can be enforced by the official tribunals of the state. Law and ethics are thus not contradictory, rather, law is that part of ethics which society has deemed fit to enforce by the instruments at its disposal.

There are moralists who maintain that the more ethical a people, the less law it needs. Does not an ancient legal maxim say, *optima est lex quae minimum relinquit arbitrio judicis* ("the best law is that which leaves the minimum to verdict of the judges") ? The ethically perfect society needs no law at all. This is also intimated in the Talmud by the following statement: "Rabbi Simlai said in the name of Rabbi Eliezar son of Rabbi Simeon: The son of David [the Messiah] will not come until all judges and officers are departed from Israel" (B. Sanhedrin 98a), implying that these will not be necessary because of the ethical relations between man and his neighbor.

For the present, however, the more of the ethical norms that a system of law includes, the higher the standards of ethical conduct it expects of its people, the higher the ethical level of these people the more ethical is that system of law. We shall find that a goodly number of ethical regulations that are quite new in the legal systems of the Occident, are practically taken for granted in the Talmud.

The Rights of the Buyer

The most obvious conclusion that one arrives at in even a superficial study of talmudic law is that it is opposed to the doctrines of *laissez faire* and *caveat emptor*. It is one of the elementary assumptions in the Talmud that even without a specific warranty the buyer is protected in his purchase and has a right to expect that the article he buys would be without defect. Maimonides, in his code, sums up this rabbinic regulation as follows: "Anyone who makes a purchase without specifying any terms does so with the intent to buy an article free from defect. If the vendor has stipulated and said: 'I sell it on condition that you do not withdraw from the sale on grounds of defect,' the vendee may nevertheless withdraw, unless he waived his right after the vendor had specified the defect of the article sold, or unless the vendee said he would accept the article with any defect that would reduce its value by such and such an amount. This provision is due to the rule that he who waives the right to a claim must know the amount of the claim and explicitly specify it, as is required in the case of overreaching." (*Mishneh Torah*, Laws Concerning Sales 15:6; See also B. Baba Mesia 51a, f.).

The buyer is protected not only against fraud and error, about which later, but also against loss by negligence of the seller, even where the seller had a legal claim for exemption. Thus the rabbis of the Talmud maintain that according to biblical law the transfer (i.e., the payment) of the purchase price from the buyer to the seller completes the sale. The rabbis, however, instituted that in addition to the payment of the price, the delivery of the purchased article was necessary in order to complete the sale. This was instituted in order to obligate the seller to exercise due care of the article he sold but still has in his possession and which is still on his premises, and, in the case of loss, not to avail himself of the claim that since payment was made, not he but the buyer, is responsible and must bear the loss. (B. Baba Mesia 47b).

As an aside, we are tempted to bring up an interesting practice that was a direct result of this rabbinic enactment. Even though the payment of the price does not complete the sale, and thus, theoretically, each party may withdraw from the deal, the rabbis felt that the transaction was binding on both in the forum of conscience, and therefore the party taking advantage of the rule of the law had to submit to an imprecation pronounced by the court invoking divine retribution against the man "who does not stand by his word." This is known as *"mi shepara"* (B. Baba Mesia 44a).

The buyer is also protected against the purchase of an article to which the seller does not have clear title. Maimonides, following the talmudic prescription, states it as follows: "One is forbidden to sell to another land or movables the title of which is disputed or upon which litigation is pending, unless he informs the buyer about it" (*Mishneh Torah*, Laws Concerning Sales 19:1).

If such disputes arise after the sale, the vendor is still held responsible. This responsibility of the seller obtains even if the contract does not specifically stipulate it. The Talmud applies to this case the principle that, "omission of the clause of guarantee by the seller is merely an error of the scribe" (B. Baba Mesia 14a). This principle covers all instances where we can reasonably assume that such a guarantee was implied even though not explicitly stated, and offers this additional protection to the buyer.

Fraud and Error

Rabbinic law is very specific about fraud. Every precaution was first taken to prevent it. One such measure of prevention was the appointment of officials to supervise and inspect weights and measures (B. Baba Batra 89b).

It was forbidden to use the same rope for the measurement of fields in the winter and in the summer (B. Baba Mesia 61b; B. Baba Batra 89b). The reason for this is that during the rainy season the rope is shorter because the wetness contracts it.

Since the vessels in which the liquids were measured had a tendency to accumulate sediment that would reduce their capacity, the

Talmud prescribes that the dealer must scour his measures and even enjoins how often the wholesaler and how often the retailer had to do it (B. Baba Batra 88a). The same applied to scales.

If fraud was commited, the aggrieved party had legal redress. In order for the law to be definite and practical, the Talmud set down the following norms: If the deception amounts to a sixth of the price, the sale is still valid but the proper adjustment in the payment must be made; if it amounts to more than a sixth, the transaction is void; if to less than a sixth, no adjustment is necessary because it is assumed that "it is the general practice to waive the right to frauds amounting to less than a sixth." (B. Baba Mesia 44b; see also Maimonides, *Mishneh Torah*, Laws Concerning Sales 12:3).

To the modern ear attuned to fixed prices, to waive one's right up to one sixth of the price jars us a bit. Whoever has done business, however, in countries where stores do not have fixed prices will find these norms more than fair. The law is fair even to the person committing the fraud, and therefore it has ruled a time limit on claims for fraud. The buyer could lodge a claim only for a time long enough to give him a chance to show the article to another merchant or to a friend who could call his attention to the fraud. This limitation of time is fair to the buyer who has the article in his possession and thus is in the position to inquire of others about its real value. If the seller is the aggrieved party the privilege of protest extends indefinitely because he does not have the article in his possession and therefore cannot show it to anyone for áppraisal (B. Baba Mesia 50b).

This regulation is followed in the Talmud by the following story to illustrate it. "The host of Rami the son of Hama sold wine and made an error. Finding him depressed, Rami asked him why he was sad. When the host answered that it was because he made an error in a sale Rami told him that he should retract. 'But' said the host, 'I tarried beyond the prescribed time—i.e., the time one can show the merchandise to a dealer or to a relative.' Thereupon Rami sent his host to Rav Nahman who told him that this time limit applied only to the buyer, but that the seller could always withdraw. Why? Because the buyer is in possession of the bought article and can show it wherever he goes so that people could tell him whether he made an error or not. The seller, however, who does not have the article in his possession cannot become aware of his error until he chances upon an article similar to his (B. Baba Mesia 51a).

These regulations apply to errors in price. If the error is in weight or measure no allowances are made. The slightest error must be rectified and there is no time limit set. (B. Baba Batra 90a). This distinction is logical and bears out our explanation about the absence of fixed prices in the commerce of those days.

An interesting sidelight on how far the rabbis opposed the *caveat emptor* principle can be observed from their emphasis upon its avoidance even where logic would suggest its tolerance. When the aggrieved party is a merchant who normally should know the value of the article he buys, we nevertheless maintain that he has the privilege of rescinding the sale. This rabbinic decision is stated by Maimonides as follows: "Just as there is fraud towards an ordinary person so is there fraud vis-à-vis a merchant, though he is an expert (Mishneh Torah, Laws Concerning Sales 12:8; see also B. Baba Mesia 51a).

We must emphasize again that the details of these rulings must be viewed in the light of the business practices of the day. It was not an era of one price commodity which was so labeled. The error had to be gross before a lay person could sense it or discover it. Some authorities have made the permissible margin larger than the sixth that we have mentioned. Thus we are told in the Talmud that Rabbi Tarfon decreed in Lod that overreaching must amount to one third of the value before the validity of the sale would be impugned. This caused the merchants to rejoice, because it was to their advantage. Then Rabbi Tarfon balanced this enactment with the further decree that the buyer could withdraw from the sale for a full day, much longer than the limited time the accepted law had permitted. The merchants then told Rabbi Tarfon that in his regulations the disadvantage outweighed the advantage and that they would therefore rather abide by the decree of the other sages (B. Baba Mesia 49b).

Deception

The Talmud extended the term, fraud, to include verbal deception even where no financial loss was involved. They called this kind of unethical conduct *geneivat da'at*, literally, "the stealing of the mind." Thus they said that one should not bargain about the price of an article if he has no intention of buying it (B. Baba Mesia 58b). Oh, how the merchants dealing in ladies' wear would appreciate the adherence to such a regulation today! One should not pretend interest in the purchase of an article when he has not the funds to buy it (ibid.). One should not sell nonkosher food as kosher even to a Gentile to whom it makes no difference (B. Hulin 94a).

The Talmud presents many similar practices that are accounted as deceptions to be avoided even if there is no financial loss caused to anyone thereby. These are unethical nevertheless because they create a false impression.

Right of Preemption

Talmudic law was very considerate of those who had priorities, priorities based not on legal claims but on a sense of justice and fairness. Talmudic law protected even such priorities with legal redress.

First we have the general exhortation not to purchase an article that someone else has put in a bid for and is considering buying. In connection with this ethical prescription this charming story is told to illustrate it.

> Rav Giddal was negotiating for a certain field, and Rav Abba went ahead and bought it. Thereupon Rav Giddal went and complained to Rav Zeira, who in turn went and complained to Rav Isaac Nappaha. "Wait until he comes to us for the Festival," said Rav Isaac Nappaha to him. When Rav Abba came he met him and asked him, "If a poor man is examining a cake and another comes and takes it away from him, what then?" "He is called a wicked man," he answered. "Then why do you, sir, act so?" he questioned him further. "I did not know that he was negotiating for it," he rejoined. "Then let him have it now," he suggested. "I will not sell it to him," he answered, "because it is the first field which I have ever bought and it is not a good omen to sell; but if he wants it as a gift, let him take it." Now Rav Giddal would not take possession of the field because it is written, *But he that hateth gifts shall live* (Proverbs 15:27). Nor would Rav Abba, because Rav Giddal had negotiated for it; and so neither took possession, and it was called "the rabbis' field" and it was used for the students of the academy (B. Kiddushin 59a).

On the basis of this passage we have the following decision in the code of Rabbi Joseph Karo: "If one seeks to buy or rent either land or movables and another person comes and buys it, he is called a *rasha,* "a wicked person" (*Hoshen Mishpat* 237:1).

The more celebrated regulations come under the caption of *dinah d'bar metsra,* "the law of the adjacent owner." The law applies to cases where we assume that a certain party has a special interest and thus has an option even without claiming it. Under this law of preemption comes the case of brothers or partners who owned property that was contiguous, and one of them sold his portion. The other brothers or partners have a right to reimburse the purchaser and remove him from the property in order to prevent a stranger from wedging into their property. (Maimonides, Mishneh Torah, Laws Concerning Neighbors 12:14; see also B. Baba Batra 22b, Baba Mesia 108a f). In this case we imply that partners and brothers have priority in the purchase if one of them wishes to sell out. The fairness of this law is quite obvious. Talmudic law goes much further, however, and extends this priority to all adjacent owners. If a man wants to sell a piece of land, his neighbor who owns the land adjacent to it has the first option to buy it. If the land was sold to another person before the neighbor had a chance to express his desire, his neighbor has a right to reimburse the buyer and remove him from the land (ibid.).

Just as noteworthy is what the Talmud cites as the source for this law. It is the biblical verse: "And thou shalt do what is right and what is good" (Deuteronomy 6:18).

The exceptions to the rule and the reasons advanced for them bespeak the ethical sensitivity of the rabbis as much as the rules themselves. The right of the adjacent owner does not apply to property bought by minor orphans and by women; not to minor orphans because "the right and the good" done to orphans in such a case exceeds that done to the adjacent owners; not to women, because it is not customary for a woman to go out and purchase, and if she did purchase, it is an act of kindness to let her retain what she has already purchased (Maimonides, Mishneh Torah, Laws Concerning Neighbors 12:13–14).

Advertising, Packaging, and Labeling

There is very much discussion today about the ethics of the current advertising, packaging, and labeling practices. It is agreed that it is wrong blatantly to misrepresent, and no one would claim that it is right to announce that an article performs functions that it does not, or that it contains ingredients that are not in it. Even though the laws forbidding these gross forms of misrepresentation are comparatively new, no one doubted that such misrepresentations were acts of deception and were ethically wrong.

Here, we are concerned with subtle psychologic misrepresentations that try to create a favorable predisposition to a commodity, a predisposition beyond the merits of the commodity. It accomplishes this purpose by innuendo, suggestion, outright claims, constant repetition, and the thousands of other tricks used in the grosser forms by the governments employing thought-control propaganda.

The strident advertising of cigarettes, beers, and toothpaste, each producer claiming that his product contains an ingredient that makes it superior to all other similar products, is that ethical?

Taking an inferior article but wrapping it in attractive containers to create an impression beyond the deserts of the commodity, is that ethically right?

Attracting customers, not by advertising the excellence and the virtues of the product, but by the distribution of gifts, prizes, bonuses, and the like, is that ethical?

Modern practice approves these methods. Nay! it considers their use as an indication of good salesmanship. Whatever means, short of fraud, you can devise to attract a customer is not only legitimate but is recommended. Not so in rabbinic law, as can be gathered clearly from the following regulations:

"One should not paint a man, or cattle, or utensils [that are for sale]" (B. Baba Mesia 60a). The idea is that these should not be painted for the purpose of making them look better than they really are. The Talmud illustrates this regulation with the following incident:

> A slave painted his face and his hair and came to Rava with the request that he purchase him. Rava, aware of the fraud, refused. The slave then approached Rav Pappa the son of Samuel, who did consent to acquire him. One day Rav Pappa asked him to bring some water. In response, the slave washed his head and his face and said to his master: "See that I am older than your father" (B. Baba Mesia 60a).

The Talmud clarifies that this prohibition applies only where the purpose is to deceive and create a false impression about the article. It relates, therefore, that Rava permitted the painting of arrows and Rav Pappa the son of Samuel permitted the painting of trees on certain articles. When asked how they granted this permission in the face of the prohibition to paint utensils, they answered that this prohibition applied only to used articles where painting created a false impression, and not to new ones where painting was merely decorative (ibid.).

In the same category is the regulation not to arrange fruit or produce in such a way that the top layer will have the best quality and thus mislead people into believing that the entire quantity is of the same quality (B. Baba Mesia 60a).

We know that not all the methods of advertising are legitimate. The trade has its own rules and regulations and has accepted a code of ethics. Among the practices considered legitimate are attracting customers by giving away gifts, prizes, and bonuses—particularly to children—and attracting customers by underselling competitors. In the Talmud, there is a difference of opinion on the subject. We quote: "Rabbi Judah said: 'A storekeeper should not distribute parched corn and nuts to children because that would develop in them the habit of coming to him. But the sages permit it. Rabbi Judah also forbids selling at less than the market price. The sages, however, said that such a one should be blessed'" (B. Baba Mesia 60a). The reason for this blessing is that he provides people their needs at a lesser expense.

The ethical standards of talmudic law are further evidenced in the principle termed *kofin al midat sedom*, i.e., "to be compelled not to act according to the manner of Sodom." One of the sins of the people of Sodom, according to the rabbis, was that they refused to do favors to others even if it cost them nothing materially and required no effort on their part. They had the attitude, described in a popular adage, of the dog in the manger. The rabbis in the Talmud applied this principle of *kofin al midat Sodom* to cases where a man, because of his rights, tried to hinder another from an act that benefited the latter and yet caused no harm to the former. For instance: A proprietor is entitled to exercise his right of exclusion even when it brings no benefit to him. Though legal, such conduct is considered unethical.

The rabbis had the tendency to make the ethical standard also the legal one. The law of the adjacent owner that we have already mentioned, is one example of the application of this attitude (B. Baba Batra 12b). The Talmud presents a concrete case to which the principle was applied. A certain person leased his mill to another for the consideration that, as rental, the lessee should grind the corn of the lessor. Subsequently the lessor became wealthy and bought another mill, and thus could do the grinding himself. He therefore demanded that the lessee now pay his rental with money instead of service. The lessee, however, preferred to continue with the original arrangement. The decision is that we compel the owner of the mill to continue with the original arrangement. The Talmud then adds the following distinction. This rule applies only if the leased mill would otherwise be idle and, thus, to make the lessee pay with money would bring a loss to him. If, however, the lessee has other orders for grinding, he may in such circumstances "be compelled not to act" in the manner of the people of Sodom," i.e., it is no loss to him to grind for others and give the money realized to the owner of the mill as rental (B. Ketubot 103a).

In the application of this principle the direction of the development of Jewish law becomes apparent. It is an effort to make the ethical, legal. Where at first we have merely a moralistic exhortation, it later develops into a legal principle (see, *Ha-Musar v'ha-Medinah b'Yisroel*, Simeon Federbush, p. 112).

Ethical Norms without Legal Force

The rabbis had a whole series of ethical rules where there were no legal sanction, and yet these were not mere exhortations, because a specific stigma expressed in a concrete manner was attached to those who violated them. We have already mentioned the institution of *mi shepara*. This concerned cases where although a man acted according to the letter of the law, his conduct was still considered unethical. The rabbis condemned these acts by saying that "the spirit of the sages is displeased with him." Verbal agreements are not legally binding, nevertheless, the spirit of the sages is displeased with him who retracts from a verbal agreement (B. Baba Mesia 48a). If a man bequeathes his property to others and nothing to his sons, his act is legally binding, but the spirit of the sages is displeased with it (B. Baba Batra 133a).

Another expression of the rabbis against the commission of an act, ethically wrong but for which there is no legal redress, is that the parties can only cherish resentment against each other. Thus if an employer charges one to hire laborers for him at a certain wage, and the agent hired them at a lower wage, the rule is that the laborers may not claim the difference since they had accepted the lower wage, but they do have a right to cherish a resentment (B. Baba Mesia 75b f; and comments of Tosafot).

Another example of this category of wrongs for which the law provides no remedy but which it expressly stigmatizes, is where the Talmud applies to him the term *rasha,* a "wicked person." Thus if one was on the point of buying a piece of property and the buyer and the seller have agreed on the price and on all the other details, the only element required for closing the transaction being the formal mode of transfer, and then a third party intervened and bought the property, the law cannot intervene, but it denounces the third party as a *rasha,* "a wicked person" (B. Kiddushin 59a).

We thus note the ethical spirit running like a thread through all the laws of the Talmud regulating the commercial relationships between man and man. These norms are not only in the realm of the purely voluntary—the only area to which, according to some philosophers, ethics can apply—but also in the area of positive law. We constantly sense the effort to make law synonymous with justice and ethics and conformable with the biblical command, "Thou shalt do that which is right and good in the eyes of the Lord" (Deuteronomy 6:18). To be sure, many of these rules and regulations cannot be applied today; the spirit which motivated them, however, is eternal.

19.   SCIENCE AND SOME ETHICAL ISSUES (1959)

In his paper *Science and Some Ethical Issues,* Professor Hudson Hoagland has touched upon three areas in which science has made great strides and at the same time created new ethical problems. The first deals with the problem of overpopulation, due directly to the increase in the life span which the progress in medical science has brought about; the second deals with the problem of eugenics, a problem which though not new has become more relevant because of the problem created by radiation due to nuclear fission; the third area concerns the propriety of the control of behavior made possible by new knowledge of the nervous system.

According to Professor Hoagland, the scientist can and should assist public decisions by helping to interpret the impact of discoveries on the broad issues of the time. Professor Hoagland, therefore, very ably marshals the facts relevant to these problems, although, contrary to his own advice, he yields to the temptation of not only marshaling the facts but also of making decisions.

We will discuss the problems presented and indicate the Jewish rabbinic sources that may shed light on them. But first, two general remarks:

The Bible says: "See, I have set before thee this day life and good, and death and evil" (Deuteronomy 10:15) ; also: "Ye shall therefore keep my statutes and my judgments, which if a man do, he shall live by them" (Leviticus 18:15).

This identification of life with the good and the keeping of the Commandments with the enhancement of life has been a cardinal principle in Judaism. The rabbis repeatedly emphasized that the words "he shall live by them" mean that God's Commandments are to be a means for the furtherance of life and not of its destruction. With the exception of three prohibitions, therefore, all Commandments of the Torah are in abeyance whenever their performance would endanger life: the proscription against public idolatry, against murder, and against adultery.

159

Jewish sources can be divided into two categories, the *halakhic* and the *'aggadic*. The Halakha is normative and expresses that which was accepted as the prescribed standard of conduct. The 'Aggadah is not normative but expresses the ideals and aspirations of the people which often went beyond the law. While not normative, the 'Aggadic affirmations do touch on ethical problems and may furnish guidance or suggest lines of development.

Overpopulation

With these as premises we shall approach the ethical problems discussed by Professor Hoagland. The first of these is the problem of overpopulation. The present threat of overpopulation is due partly to the advances made by medical science. Whereas in the past, the high rate of infant mortality, the frequency of epidemics, and the existence of many ailments that were fatal or incurable, reduced the pace of population growth, today these have been eliminated as factors. As a result population growth is so rapid that it is easy to envisage a saturation point. The increased effort to enlarge food production can only postpone this day but cannot eliminate it. He quotes Murray Luck who says: "The battle between production and reproduction will never be won by production alone."

Even before this saturation point is reached, however, there are obvious dangers. When jobs and educational opportunities are lacking, youth easily becomes victim to demogogues and revolutionary leaders. Overcrowding leads to a lower standard of living with its consequent evils. Rightly does Professor Hoagland claim that population pressure is a powerful aid to communism and demogogic dictatorship, and that may be a primary contribution to the ultimate immorality of a nuclear world war.

There is therefore the imperative to limit population. Medical science fortunately has also produced correctives that could help limit population growth, the latest of these being oral contraceptives taken in the form of pills. Science, however, can only make inventions available, says Professor Hoagland. These will come to nothing if religious and social tabus prevent their use. The reference, we surmise, is to the objection from certain religious quarters to "artificial" and "unnatural" means of interfering with purposes of nature. What has Jewish tradition to say on the subject?

These terms are not in the vocabulary of the Jewish tradition.

To be sure, procreation and the propagation of the race are a biblical commandment. The verse, "Be fruitful and multiply" (Genesis 1:28), the rabbis of the Talmud count as a positive commandment. Nevertheless, this does not preclude the permission of birth control. The Talmud actually prescribes the use of contraceptives in certain cases. Thus, the Talmud says:

> Rabbi Bebai recited before Rabbi Nahman: Three categories of women may use [according to some versions, *must* use] an absorbent during marital intercourse: a minor, a pregnant woman, and a nursing woman. The minor, because otherwise she might become pregnant and as a result might die; a pregnant woman, because otherwise she might cause her foetus to degenerate into a *sandal* (a fish-shaped abortion due to super-fetation); a nursing woman, because otherwise she might have to wean her child prematurely because of a second conception and this would result in its death (B. Yebamot 12a).

According to this dictum of the Talmud the use of contraception is permitted [and prescribed] when there is a danger of harm to an unborn child, or to a child already born, or to the mother.

Under normal circumstances the use of contraceptives is forbidden, not for the reason that it is an unnatural act and therefore immoral, but because it prevents the performance of the commandment implied in the biblical verse, "Be fruitful and multiply" (Genesis 1:28). The commandment is violated not only by the use of contraceptives but also by the practice of absolute self-restraint or total abstinence (Eben ha-Ezer 76). This objection, however, applies only until such a time that a person will have fulfilled this commandment, i.e., after he has sired two male children according to the school of Shammai, or a male and a female child according to the school of Hillel. The opinion is also worth mentioning that in a year of famine one is forbidden to have children (B. Ta'anit 11a).

If there is room for doubt as to whether the use of contraceptives is permissible when it concerns planned parenthood, there can be no doubt that it is permitted where the absence of its use will bring the evils accompanying overpopulation.

Natural Selection

The second problem created by the advance in medical science is that it interferes with the process of natural selection. Whereas in the past natural selection has eliminated people with defective genes and given them no chance to live to maturity, modern medicine enables such persons to live to maturity and thus neutralizes the effects of natural selection. The accumulation of such defects may lead to the lowering of the standard of fitness of humanity as a whole. As René J. Dubos of the Rockefeller Institute of Medical Research said at the annual convention of the National Congress of Parents and Teachers, "For the first time in the history of living things we are allowing the survival of biological misfits many of whom will become a burden for society. Even more significant is the fact that all kinds of hereditary defects that used to be rapidly eliminated by evolutionary selection are now being reproduced in our communities. . . . While the preservation of human life is demanded by moral, social, and religious considerations, we are now engaged in a process which may result in ultimate dangers. . . . This policy may constitute a step towards social suicide, however noble it may appear in the light of our religious convictions and present-day ethics" (*New York Times,* May 20, 1958).

This problem of the survival of the unfit is aggravated by current nuclear testing. Radiation resulting from these tests has the double effect of producing sicknesses of various kinds and at the same time of effecting changes in the genes that will adversely affect an appreciable number of progeny of the people thus affected.

This poses two problems; (1) Would it be permissible to sterilize the people thus affected in order to prevent the birth of defective children? (2) Is it ethical to have nuclear tests when we know that thousands of individuals will suffer crippling genetic damage which will be transmitted to future generations? This damage has to be weighed against the advantage of having an atomic stalemate as a deterrent to nuclear war.

The first question is broader as it covers a larger territory. Whereas it is estimated that from the people who are alive today who will give birth to one and a half billion babies, thirty million will be born with serious congenital defects inherited over generations of defective genes, only 6000 of these will be due to radiation from fall-out. This number will of course increase as the use of atomic power whether for peace or war purposes increases. For the present, however, this is a small percentage of the total.

The science of eugenics could come to the rescue with measures to reduce the number of defectives that our medical progress helped to survive. Professor Hoagland suggests the use of sterilization as well as of artificial insemination. On the use of both of these the rabbinic sources have much to say.

We shall preface our comments with the observation that we already find in the Talmud certain eugenical principles. The Talmud believed in heredity and therefore urged that in the choosing of a mate this should be kept in mind. Thus we find the advice in the Talmud: "A tall man should not marry a tall woman lest their children be lanky. A short man should not marry a short woman lest their children be dwarfish. A fair man should not marry a fair woman lest their children be excessively fair.

A dark man should not marry a dark woman lest their children be excessively swarthy." (B. Bekhorot 45b) They emphasized this principle of heredity, not only as to physical characteristics, but also as to the mental and the spiritual. Thus they advise: "A man should sell all he possesses with the object of marrying the daughter of a learned man, for if he were to die or be exiled, his children would be learned; and he should not take as a wife the daughter of an unlearned man, for if he were to die or be exiled his children will be ignorant. A man should sell all he possesses with the object of marrying the daughter of a scholar or giving his daughter in marriage to a scholar. This is like uniting grapes of the vine to grapes of the vine, which is good and acceptable. But let him not marry the daughter of an ignoramus, because that is like uniting grapes of the vine to berries of the bush, which is something ugly and unacceptable" (B. Pesahim 49a).

There are three purposes for which sterilization is usually advocated:

(1) therapeutic, where childbirth may hurt the mother;
(2) eugenic, where the birth will result in a defective child;
(3) punitive, where the sexual activity will hurt society directly as in the case of sex offenders (Joseph Fletcher, *Morals and Medicine*, Princeton, 1954, p. 145).

Of these three, only the first two come within the purview of our problem. On the first problem rabbinic teachings are very clear. Where childbirth would be fatal to the mother, not only sterilization, but also abortion is permitted. Thus the rabbis say: "If a woman is in hard travail, one cuts up the child in her womb and

brings it forth member by member, because her life comes before
the life of the child. But if the greater part has proceeded forth,
one may not touch it, for one may not set aside one person's life
for that of another" (Ahalot 7:6).

This decision the rabbis base on the principle that the taking of
a life is punishable only when it is the life of a child after birth, as
the rule is also in common law. There is this difference, however.
In common law, birth means the complete extrusion from the body;
but in Jewish law, birth is defined as the extrusion of the greater
part of the child from the body of the mother. (According to one
source, if the head comes first, the extrusion of the greater part of
the head is accounted as birth).

This certainly implies that in an ectopic pregnancy the surgical
removal of the foetus is permissible because, before birth, the child
is *pars viscerum matris* or, to use talmudic terminology, the foetus
is accounted as the thigh of the mother, and there is no objection to
sacrificing a limb for a complete life.

What do the rabbis teach about the prevention of pregnancy
through sterilization when pregnancy would bring harm to the
mother? The following incident related in the Talmud will suggest
an answer:

> Judah and Hezekiah were twins. The features of one were
> developed at the end of nine months, and those of the other
> were developed at the beginning of the seventh month. Judith,
> the wife of Rabbi Hiyya [and the mother of Judah and He-
> zekiah] having suffered in consequence agonizing pains at
> childbirth, changed her clothes [disguised herself] on recovery
> and appeared before Rabbi Hiyya. "Is a woman," she asked,
> "commandeed to propagate the race?" "No," he replied. And
> relying on this decision she drank a sterilizing potion (B.
> Yebamot 65b).

The talmudic term for this potion is *ikrin*. Medical science has not
verified what this cup of *ikrin* was. The principle is nevertheless
implicit that in cases where pregnancy is accompanied by pain the
woman is allowed to submit to sterilization. This permission in the
case of the woman is based on the principle declared in the Mishnah
that: A man is commanded concerning the duty of propagation but
not the woman (ibid.).

To press the problem further: Is such sterilization permissible when no harm or pain to the mother is involved? In other words, is it permissible when the purpose is not therapeutic, but let us say, eugenic?

Another rabbinic source makes this flat statement: "A man is not allowed to drink a sterilizing potion in order to prevent him from causing pregnancy, but a woman is permitted to drink a sterilization potion in order to prevent her becoming pregnant" (Tosefta Yebamot 8:2).

The later authorities are divided whether this permission is unconditional. All agree that if the sterilization has been done to prevent conception in the case of a woman who suffers great pain when giving birth, it is permitted. Where there is no pain these authorities permit it only after the obligation to propagate the race has already been fulfilled, i.e., if she has already given birth to a male and female child, according to the school of Hillel, or two male children, according to the school of Shammai.

If the children already born are delinquent and the woman is afraid that those to be born would follow suit, there is at least one authority that would sanction sterilization. The reason given is that the fear of bringing delinquent children into the world is a more valid ground for the prevention of conception than pain accompanying birth. (See *Pit'hei Teshuvah to Eben ha-Ezer* 7:12 quoting the opinion of Solomon Luria, 1510–1573.)

An 'Aggadic statement in the Talmud would suggest the opposite. The Talmud reports an imaginary conversation between the Prophet Isaiah and King Hezekiah. To the prophet's rebuke for his failure to have children the king answers in his own defense that he had foreseen, by the help of the Holy Spirit, that the children that would issue from his loins would not be virtuous. To this the Prophet replied: "What have you to do with the secrets of the All-Merciful? You should have done what you were commanded, and let the Holy One blessed be He, do that which pleases Him" (B. Berakhot 10a).

It would seem then that at least as far as the sterilization of the woman is concerned there is no objection, if the purpose is the health of the mother or the welfare of society.

What about the sterilization of the male of the species? The talmudic sources forbid it categorically. The only exception is when it is necessary for health reasons. This strictness in the case of the male is perhaps due to the abuses of the practice in ancient times. First, it usually involved the mutilation of the body. It was also practiced in order to raise eunuchs, a widespread practice in ancient times abhorrent to the biblical legislator (Deuteronomy 23:2).

Would this also preclude the modern method of sterilization where there is no real visible mutilation of the body? The statement quoted above from the Tosefta seems to forbid any form of sterilization in the case of the male. And yet, some later authorities have permitted it in some cases. When there is danger to life or even a suspicion of danger, we operate on the well-established principle that saving a life supersedes all other considerations (see *Otzar ha-Posekim*, v. I, p. 126). There is also a strange suggestion made by one talmudic commentator that if a man wishes to eliminate his sex urge (evidently in order to avoid temptation) he may do so, provided he has already fulfilled the obligation to propagate the race. He adds that he had actually heard of some distinguished scholars who drank a sterilizing potion for that purpose (comment of RITBO on B. Yebamot 63b) in order to be able to pursue their scholarly occupation without disturbance. It would not be stretching the point very much, if we should practice it for males where sterilization would prevent the disturbance of society.

Artificial Insemination

As a eugenic measure Professor Hoagland suggests that future generations may not find it abhorrent to practice artificial insemination, not only in cases of sterile husbands, but also in the case of normal people who will use artificial insemination in order to make it possible for illustrious people to sire a greater number of offspring and thus "improve the breed" of humanity. This may even be extended to include illustrious men long dead but whose sperm it is now possible to preserve in deep freeze.

This goes far beyond the current implications of the problem. Recently the question has received much attention in the general press of England because of a court case in which the legitimacy of a child born of artificial insemination was questioned (see *Manchester Guardian Weekly* for January and February 1958).

As practiced at present artificial insemination is used mostly in cases of infertility of the husband. There are two methods: AIH, where the semen of the husband is used for artificial insemination, and AID, where the semen of a donor is used. AIH is tried in cases of impotence and other physical difficulties that prevent normal fertilization, and where the quantity and quality of the husband's sperm cells is substandard. AID is used mainly in the following cases:

(1) where the husband is irremediably sterile, according to present knowledge;
(2) where there have been one or more *rhesus* tragedies in the family;
(3) where the husband is the carrier of some severe inherited disability;
(4) somewhat theoretically, as a means of improving the stock by using donors of outstanding mental and physical attributes (Dr. Margaret Jackson, "Report of Royal Society of Medicine," *Manchester Guardian Weekly*, January 16, 1958).

Professor Hoagland would be interested mostly in the last instance where the main purpose is "improving the breed." We, however, shall have to treat the total picture in order to get the Jewish view on the matter. The question of artificial insemination has been treated extensively in modern halakhic literature. It touches upon family life and morality and is therefore of great concern. Most recently it was treated exhaustively in the first volume of a new *Annual* devoted to questions of Jewish law (*Noam*, V. I.).

We divided the question of artificial insemination into AIH and AID. In the case of AIH the only objection to the practice is that artificial insemination is an unnatural act forbidden on the grounds of Onanism. The consensus of opinion of the Jewish authorities is that since this discharge, though not the result of natural intercourse is used for purposes of conception, it cannot be called Onanism (*Otzar ha-Posekim*, vol. I, p. 12).

In the case of AID there are greater objections. Joseph Fletcher enumerates the following:

(1) it is unnatural as the breeding of test-tube babies in a laboratory by nonhuman chemicals. It is like stud-breeding;
(2) it is a sin against the laws of nature since the husband's copula is absent and yet essential to a lawful conception;

(3) it is an injustice to the offspring because, being adulterous, it makes bastards of the children resulting therefrom (Fletcher, *Morals and Medicine*, p. 116).

To us the main question is the third. Does AID violate the law against adultery, and are the children resulting therefrom, therefore, illegitimate? The legal aspect of the question is based entirely on the discussion in the Talmud regarding a woman who became pregnant from bathing in a bathtub in which the man who had bathed before her left a seminal discharge from which she became pregnant. The talmudic ruling is that the child is considered legitimate (B. Hagigah 15a).

Whether such a pregnancy is possible, medically speaking, is irrelevant. In principle, we have here a primitive form of a case of AID. The principle derived from it is also applicable to the modern scene. The question we face is that in the talmudic case insemination was incidental and without the woman's consent, while in the case of AID it is planned and has the woman's consent. Opinions differ as to whether we should make this distinction. The later authorities, while forbidding the practice, deduced the principle that there is no adultery without physical intercourse. It is the act of cohabitation that is forbidden, an act absent in artificial insemination (see *Noam*, pp. 119 ff.).

This at least removes the stigma of adultery from those who have submitted to artificial insemination, and the stigma of illegitimacy from the children born therefrom. Adultery and illegitimacy apply only to cases where there is lust, broken faith, and physical intercourse. Jewish tradition is thus at variance with those persuasions that condemn all artificial insemination as unnatural and therefore forbidden, as well as with those that permit AIH while condemning AID as adulterous.

That does not mean, however, that Jewish authorities permit AID. There are a number of other considerations legal and moral that complicate matters. There is the question of the legal paternity of the child. There is also the question of the possibility of mating brothers with sisters. (For other considerations see Fletcher, *Morals and Medicine*, pp. 129 ff.) If these considerations should cause us concern for the family with a totally sterile husband, we can find solace in a report of the Israel Medical Association which tells of a new method of insemination developed by Dr. Rozin of the Hadassah Hospital in Jerusalem. This would make it possible even for a sterile husband to become a true biological father and would avoid many of the complex legal and religious problems involved (See *Israel Digest,* May 16, 1958, p. 6.) because the husband supplies the fluid while the donor gives cell-free plasma that acts as a chemical aid (booster) to fertilization.

Nuclear Testing

In view of the evil effects of radiation, we are confronted with the question of the morality of nuclear testing. We know that radiation is harming many people and is victimizing many more by imposing crippling genetic damage that will be transmitted to future generations. In defense of the tests, Professor Hoagland presents the advantage of an atomic stalemate which is a deterrent to nuclear war. Is it not reasonable to request that we sacrifice these comparatively few people for the sake of saving humanity? The number of the people affected is, according to Professor Hoagland, negligible compared with the total number of children born defective due to other causes. In passing, we may mention that the number quoted by Professor Hoagland is much smaller than the estimate given by other scientists. Linus Pauling, for instance, said: ". . . Accordingly, we may say that the predicted effect of carbon 14 released in these bomb tests will be to produce about one million defective children and about two million embryonic neonatal deaths, and that the predicted effects of other isotopes will be somewhat smaller" (*The New York Times,* May 8, 1958).

From the ethical point of view each human being is important, and the fact that, comparatively speaking, only a small number is involved does not make it less of a crime. The ethical question is, do we have the right to make some people suffer to save others? There is the well-known principle in the Talmud that if your life is threatened you have the right to save yourself by killing the assailant first (B. Sanhedrin 72a). This is the human right of self-defense. There is also the law of the "pursuer," i.e., if a man is pursuing another man with the intent to kill him all those present are obligated to save the pursued, even if it involves the taking the pursuer's life (Maimonides, *Mishneh Torah,* Laws Concerning the Murderer 1:6.). And at the same time the Talmud enjoins: "If one was pursuing his fellow to slay him and he could have been saved by maiming the limb of the pursuer but did not thus save himself, killing him instead, he is executed on this account" (B. Sanhedrin 74a). The only time we are entitled to kill is to prevent an assailant from killing us or killing another human being. If, however, a man tells me to kill another man or he would kill me, the rabbis rule that he should rather allow himself to be killed (B. Pesahim 25a). An even clearer case is the following: "If people walking on the road are accosted by an enemy and given the choice to deliver one of their number for death lest all be killed, they should rather all submit to death rather than deliver one of their number" (P. Terumot 8:10; see also amazing responsum of Rabbi Yoel ben Samuel Serkes (Bah) on an actual case called Responsum on Surrender, translation and analysis by Rabbi Elijah J. Schochet).

Some apologists for the test tell us that there are victims in all progress. Thousands of people die in automobile accidents, but no one suggests that we stop manufacturing autos. The same is true of air travel. Furthermore, in war do we not sacrifice one part of the population to save the other? None of those comparisons can stand the test of logic. In all these cases the people who suffer are involved. The victims are also participants, they are not innocent bystanders. Furthermore, the suffering is not inevitable. There need not be casualties in automobile travel. In the case of atomic testing it is inevitable. Radiation always produces ill effects. Moreover, the sin committed is so grievous because the defects are transmitted to future generations. The crime against the unborn cannot be condoned on any of these grounds. We even question whether nuclear testing can prevent war. Experience has not borne out this thesis. The disturbing thing is that in these affairs action never waits for ethical considerations. All we can ask, actually, is that atomic testing be stopped, at least temporarily, until some safer ways of testing can be found.

Changing Personality

The last problem posed in Professor Hoagland's study is the question of the temporary or permanent change in the behavior patterns of men and women. Those who oppose it claim that such therapy is inconsistent with our concept of the dignity of man. Also, since the practice has become associated with Chinese "brain-washing" and

Soviet "confessions" it has become unsavory to us. It constitutes a dangerous tool which we are tempted to use for evil purposes.

And yet the legal principle of *abusus non tollit usum* ought to warn us against such an attitude. If the practice has a useful purpose and can be morally justified we should not leave it to the immoral uses of criminals and we should not be deterred from employing it for beneficial purposes. Actually the same problem is present in curing physical ailments. In addition to the fact that many major physical operations also change the personality of a human being, there were objections in some quarters even to orthodox medical cures. Where treatment necessitated mutilation it was considered "inconsistent with the dignity of man." Where no mutilation was involved it was considered by some religious sects to be an interference with the Will of God.

The Talmud, in commenting on the verse, "only he shall pay for the loss of his time, and shall cause him to be thoroughly healed" (Exodus 21:19), says: "From here we infer that the physician is given permission to heal" (B. Berakhot 61a). The code of R. Joseph Karo is even more emphatic. It says: "The Torah gave permission to the physician to heal. It is a religious commandment and is indeed included in the obligation to save life. . . . If the physician refrains from healing, he is guilty of shedding blood. (*Yoreh De'ah* 361:1). This emphasis was necessary because evidently there were people who disagreed. Such an opinion is found in the commentary on the Bible of R. Moses ben Nahman (1195–1270). He said that illness was a punishment from God and a person should allow it to run its course. The only concession we make is that the physician *may* practice his art on him. (See commentary of Ramban on Leviticus 26:11. I am indebted to Professor Saul Lieberman for calling my attention to this comment.)

A clearer intimation of such an attitude is found in an earlier rabbinic source:

> It happened that Rabbi Ishmael and Rabbi Akiba were strolling in the streets of Jerusalem. Another man was with them. They encountered a sick person who said to them, "My masters, tell me wherewith should I be healed?" They told him to take such and such until a cure would be effected. Thereupon the person who was with them started this conversation:
>
> "Who afflicted this man with sickness?"

"The Holy One blessed be He."

"And you people presume to interfere in an area that is not yours. He afflicted and you heal?"

"What is your occupation?"

"I am a tiller of the soil, as you can see by the sickle in my hands."

"Who created the field and the vineyard?"

"The Holy One blessed be He."

"And you dare to trespass into an area not yours? He created these and you eat their fruit?"

"Don't you see the sickle in my hand? Should I not go out and plow the field, cover it, fertilize it, weed it, nothing would grow!"

"Fool," the Rabbis concluded, "could you not infer from your occupation that which is written, "as for man his days are as grass" (Psalms 103:39). Just as with a tree if it is not fertilized, plowed, and weeded it does not grow. Even if it already grew but then is not watered it dies; so the body is like the tree, the fertilizer is the medicine, and the farmer is the doctor" (Midrash Shmuel 4:1).

In this charming parable we have an intimation of an attitude instructive for our case. Whatever improves upon nature does not interfere with nature nor is inconsistent with the dignity of man. Jewish tradition corroborates the affirmation of Joseph Fletcher when he said: "We may affirm our first principle that the moral stature of man, the truly human status, is measured by his knowledge of his circumstances, including physical nature, and by his ability to control those circumstances towards chosen rather than fully determined ends" (Fletcher, *Morals and Medicine*, p. 93).

Man's right to improve nature is brought out even more explicitly in a conversation the Talmud reports to have taken place between the scholar Rabbi Akiba and the Roman Procurator Tineus Rufus. The Roman asked Rabbi Akiba whose handiwork was more beautiful, man's or God's. Rabbi Akiba unhesitatingly answered that man's work was more beautiful and brought in several examples of raw material and its finished product as proof (Midrash Tanhuma, Tazria 5). Just as we welcome improvement in the physical constitution of man, we should also welcome it in his mental and spiritual constitution. If this change in his personality is not used for evil purposes but to help a person, why should it not be encouraged?

Jewish tradition views man as a co-worker with God in the process of creation.

Rabbi J. J. Cohen in his book *The Case of Religious Naturalism* draws a contrast between Taoism and Judaism on this point. Whereas Taoism teachers ". . . 'therefore the perfect is nothing, the great Sage takes no action. In doing this, he follows the pattern of the universe,' Judaism assigned to man the role of partnership with God" (p. 91). Is it not true that a change of personality takes place when a person undergoes a serious operation? A change of personality takes place when a person goes through a religious "conversion." When we urge a person to repent, are we not telling him to change his personality? We are aware that there is a difference. In these cases the change is incidental, a by-product, while in the treatment of mental cases it is sought directly. Yet, the main purpose in both cases is the healing of the person, and on that basis we should permit it in all cases.

Conclusion

The ethical questions that we have discussed all touch upon the improvement of our lives. Scientific discoveries have put at our disposal certain means which we can use for that purpose. Professor Hoagland assigns to the scientist the role of the discoverer of knowledge. This knowledge is neutral. Decision concerning its use must be made by others. Whether the scientist can continue to occupy this neutral position, is a moot question. The tone of the last chapter of Professor Hoagland also points in that direction. When the discoveries of the scientist have the power to destroy mankind and there are powers that are tempted to use them thus, can the scientist plead innocence?

Professor Hoagland complains that certain religious groups or certain religious tenets have blocked the way for the beneficial use of some scientific discoveries and suggests [in the name of David Finn] that theologians should consider it their task, "to make acceptable the necessary conduct of individuals so as to implement these values [of science] and preserve man against himself." What Professor Hoagland has missed is that the values he refers to are no more than the eagerness for physical comforts and security without question of direction and purpose. Apropos of this Dr. Jerals C. Brauer said:

To be sure, it is good that man constantly enlarges his knowledge and his control over nature. But what is the purpose of this? Merely to extend our physical lives, to be more comfortable, to eat better, to travel more rapidly, or to have a greater variety of recreation? Is this the true end of this marvelous creature called man?

If man loses his vision of the ultimate meaning of life, he loses everything, even if he creates a bright brave new world. What will it profit us if we gain a whole new world through atomic energy but lose our souls? As religion faces the atomic age, it must keep such questions and its faith before the people. Without this vision the people will perish." (Jerals G. Brauer, *Tower Topics,* University of Chicago, March 1958 p. 4.)

Thus, perhaps man has to be preserved against himself, but also against the self which science helps to make him. If the above should be considered the language of a theologian (Dr. Brauer is Dean of the Federated Theological Faculty), we may quote a renowned scientist who spoke similarly "way back" in 1946. A. V. Hill, a leading physiologist said:

What scientists today need is the inspiration of a great ideal, a common interest, a common standard of ethical behavior, a common refusal to sacrifice or exploit a universal good for a temporary or sectional advantage. How can we achieve it? Only the future can show, but it is worth trying. . . . But the truest form of realism is to recognize that human well-being, indeed the continued existence of human society depends more on the improvement of morality and reasonableness than on invention of machinery or organization. (Quoted by Professor Judah Goldin in a lecture at Iowa State University. See *Reconstructionist,* Jan. 10, 1947, p. 10.)

We agree with Professor Hoagland that theologians should be concerned with the findings of science as much as with Graeco-Roman and Judaic traditions, as indeed they are. The mistake, however, is that the scientific findings, according to Professor Hoagland, are neutral, and the theologian has to start with, "It has been told thee, O man, what is good, and what doth the Lord require of thee" (Micah 6:8). For this we have to go to a system of values inherent in a tradition. The new scientific discoveries confront the theologians with new problems and new applications which must be defined. They may modify or change some aspect of the tradition and shed new light upon it. But it is the tradition that must furnish the "great ideal" that A. V. Hill claims that even the scientist needs. It is only in that way that the scientist and the theologians will be able to work jointly for the good of humanity.

20. THE WORD OF GOD

Jewish life has been subjected to a series of shocks, of which the present shock is merely the culmination. Whenever a crisis occurred in Jewish life, the faithful consoled themselves with the belief that with the coming of the Messiah and the establishment of a Jewish commonwealth all the ills that living as a minority in hostile surroundings bred would be cured. Now, when this devoutly wished for consummation has been achieved, perhaps not in the way we dreamed of and hoped and prayed for, we find that not only has it not solved all the problems we faced as a minority, but has created new, and in some instances, more serious ones, which, some claim, may in the long run threaten our future in the diaspora more seriously. This crisis so challengingly presented by Professor Mordecai Kaplan may be summerized by a comment made by the rabbis on the following verse:

> Behold the days will come, saith the Lord God
> That I will send a famine in the land,
> Not a famine of bread, nor a thirst for water
> But of hearing the words of the Lord.
>
> (Amos 8:11)

Upon this verse the rabbis made the following comment: The words of the Lord, this is the End; the words of the Lord, this is prophecy; the words of the Lord, this the Halakha (B. Shabbat 138b). The words of the Lord for which according to the prophet there will be a hunger, the rabbis interpret to refer to the End of Days, i.e., the Messianic era, to the reappearance of prophecy, and to Halakha.

Without stretching the meaning of these terms too far even homiletically we may interpret them to mean: the end (*keitz*) refers to status, what should be our status outside the State of Israel? prophecy (*nevu'ah*), ideology, what will be the central ideology that will unite the Jews of the world? and Halakha, what should be our attitude to Halakha?

176

To me it is clear and evident that the challenge to Jewish life in America will have to be met on these three fronts.

STATUS

The question of Jewish status is not new in our history; it appeared every time the Jews settled in a new country. It was, however, the change of status that came with the advent of the period of emancipation that, according to Professor Kaplan, was the first great challenge to the survival of the Jew. The preemancipation status of the Jew, with all its cruel discrimination, had the one great effect of making the corporate Jewish community possible and necessary. The powers that be dealt with the Jew, not directly as an individual, but as a member of the community. The individual Jew thus came into contact with the body politic of the land wherein he lived only indirectly, through the instrumentality of the community. He was, therefore, completely dependent on the Jewish community, and the community compensated him for this lack of a native land by giving him the feeling of belonging in spite of being in exile. With the advent of emancipation, the Jew was allowed to establish contact with the country in which he lived and its government, without the mediation of the Jewish community. This weakened the structure of the Jewish community and also created the problem of defining the status of the Jew. The emancipated Jew could no longer think in terms of exile and redemption, since he was now a citizen of the land where he lived with equal rights and obligations, at least theoretically. The function of the Jewish community shrank and, to many, became superfluous. The various answers and adjustments, their successes and failures, are now a matter of history.

With the establishment of the State of Israel, the problem was revived but with a new twist. Arthur Koestler's renunciation of his membership in the Jewish people has focused attention upon the new phase of the problem. Now that there is a Jewish state, what makes one who is not a citizen of that state, a Jew? Will one have to settle in Israel if he wants to maintain his Jewishness as Arthur Koestler maintains? What is now the bond that will unite the Jews of the world? Or, are we destined to become a number of tribes?

Professor Kaplan suggests that we adopt the term peoplehood as describing the status of the Jew most adequately. Perhaps we should adopt this on the advice of Jewish folklore that—*shinui hashem segulah l'arikhat yamim*—the changing of one's name acts like a charm and promotes longevity. Peoplehood is like a large tent that covers a great deal of territory, and let us add, a multitude of sins as well. The prophet has already said that when one enlarges his tent he must lengthen his ropes and strengthen his stakes (Isaiah 54:2). The question is what are the ropes that we are going to lengthen and the stakes that we are going to strengthen?

PROPHECY

This brings us to our second question, that of *nevu'ah*, prophecy. Prophecy has always appeared as a beacon light to the people of Israel. The words of the prophets quickened their flagging spirits in periods of exile and distress, and challenged them when they felt at ease. There is lacking in our midst today a great idea that would galvanize the people. Our secularism is the result rather than the cause of it. As Professor Salo Baron has properly said: "On the whole, secularism thrives on indifference and negation."

To the preceding generation *shivat tzion* ("the return to Zion") and *binyan ha-aretz* ("the rebuilding of the land") were dreams and visions that gave our people spirit and ambition and hope. In our generation, the concern for our brethren overseas, the magnificent and glorious efforts to aid the survivors of the gas chambers and the crematoria, put compassion and enthusiasm into the hearts of the Jews of America.

The time is approaching when neither of these will offer any motive power nor dramatize the oneness of the Jewish people, neither for the masses nor for the intellectual elite. Ideals cannot be created to order by the campaign departments of big organizations nor by the public relations departments of seminaries or fraternal organizations. Propaganda will not create ideals of enduring value. These must emanate from a great teacher or a great thinker, from a person of great moral leadership. Who shall conceive the great idea, who shall speak the right word that will find its way into the hearts of men? The people are ready for it; the thinking people are searching for it.

If a new devotion to religious values is to be the answer, then some new emphasis on the analogy of the birth of the Hassidic movement has to come to the fore that will answer a deeply felt need of the Jew of today. The new interest in theology, not only among the clergy, but also among the intelligent laity here and in Israel, may be a straw in the wind. The fact that among us Jews the writers on theology come mainly from the laity is of significance. Let us hope that the words of the Lord for which we are searching may emerge from their midst.

It is clear that this problem faces not only the Jews of America but also the Jews of Israel. While Israeli Jews are not threatened with assimilation, they are most certainly threatened by secularism and a consequent threat of separatism. If some unifying idea will not be found, then even if the Jews in their respective countries find some rallying point of their own, we shall cease to be the Children of Israel, but will rather become a series of tribes as some Jewish sociologists claim we already are. As long as the present generation of Israelis continue to live there shall be a common memory with the diaspora Jews. With the rise of the new generation in Israel to whom the *galut* will not be even a memory but something they may study about in history books, they will be hard put to find a common basis for peoplehood.

This problem, therefore, faces the people of Israel as much as those who live outside Israel. I have spoken to a number of people in Israel regarding this question and received various answers, each answering according to the ideology he subscribed to Some, of course, insisted that every Jew who wanted to continue to be a Jew must settle in Israel. Among those who did not take this view there was a great deal of emphasis on the cultural ties that would have to exist between Israel and American Jewry. Cultural ties, however, cannot exist in a vacuum. Will there be a Jewish cultural life in America strong enough to be even on the receiving side of the culture created in Israel? The present realities do not make us too hopeful in that direction. A member of the Ministry of Religion to whom I had spoken at length told me that they had a department in the ministry whose function was to keep in contact with the diaspora communities. These contacts were based squarely on the assumption that there will be a religious community of interest between Israel and the Jews outside of Israel. To these people, Israel will still be the Holy Land because of past memories and because to them it is only in Israel that Jewish life can be lived to its maximum. I am not at all concerned with the complaint about the stranglehold that the extremists are alleged to have on religious life in Israel. Life will take care of that. Nor am I concerned with the lament that some American rabbis would not have a right to function in Israel. Perhaps it is well to remind some American rabbis forcefully that there are certain traditions we American rabbis have discarded, but that others still hold sacred. I have great faith that both problems will eventually iron themselves out because life is stronger than all the forces that are opposing it. It may take a little time and we must be patient. The quest for *nevu'ah* on this front will have to be a cooperative effort between Israel and the diaspora.

HALAKHA

Professor Louis Ginzberg once said that whereas the words of the prophets are like flames of fire, the rabbis of the talmudic period were more successful in their work of disseminating the word of God than were the prophets, and they were the ones who became the great educators of the people who molded its character through the Halakha and established a pattern of life that was the norm for *k'lal Yisroel* up to the recent past. Today, these norms, even where still professed, are honored more in the breach than in the observance. Hence our third quest for the words of God is in the field of Halakha. Among the faithful there are now stirrings regarding the Halakha and there is a great desire to make it operative again. Even in the camp of Reform Jews there is a desire to reestablish a minimum code of observance, where before it was cut out root and branch. In our group, the law committee has been unusually active. The Orthodox brethren seek the reestablishment of the Sanhedrin. All these spell a desire to make the Halakha operative once more in our lives.

Many of the members of the Conservative movement who stress the adherence to the traditional religious observances and sincerely desire to revive adherence to the Halakha, express their dilemma in the talmudic idiom: *Oi li miyotzri v'oi li m'yitzri* ("woe unto me from my Creator and woe unto me from my (evil) inclination"; or, *Oi li im omar v'oi li im lo omar* ("woe unto me if I speak and woe unto me if I do not speak"). On the one hand we realize that all is not well and that things cannot go on as they are now; on the other hand we are apprehensive that some of the suggested changes will leave us *kore-ah mikan u-mikan* ("bald on both sides") : Those who did not observe until now shall continue on their own path, while those who did observe will become confused. It is not always that the Talmud applies the adage, *eilu v'eilu divrei Elohim hayim* ("both are the words of the living God"), when there is a difference of opinion. It is applied specifically to the differences of opinion between Hillel and Shamai. In the case of the differences among their disciples, however, the Talmud laments: Ever since the number of disciples of Hillel and Shamai who were not sufficiently trained increased, the number of conflicts increased and the Torah became like two Torahs" (B. Sotah 47b).

One of the great difficulties we encounter when we deal with Jewish law in America is the fact that we operate practically, in a vacuum. The people with whom we deal have drifted away completely from Jewish observance. The question is not whether to eliminate certain religious restrictions, or to ease certain severities of the law, but rather whether there should be any law at all. Shabbes has been one of the first casualties of the laxity that prevails in religious observance. Our law committee, in its desire to bolster the observance of Shabbat, has sought to find ways and means of bringing the observance up to date. One of the means was to permit travel on the Sabbath when it was for the purpose of attending services at the synagogue. Today Jews live in scattered areas and it would be hard for each one to reside within walking distance of the synagogue. The irony of it is that we Jews in America live today in far compacter masses than ever before in our history. It is our desire to pray that has diminished, and the reluctance to make an effort to go to the synagogue has increased.

Our modern civilization, with its overemphasis upon comfort and the general amenities of life, has made Jews and non-Jews alike a rather easygoing lot. How would our fathers, living in an age of faith, have reacted to such a problem? They would have said that it was not always to the best interest of religion to have a large synagogue or to have a large attendance at the services. Wherever ten Jews gather they form a *minyan*. Of course ten men cannot engage a rabbi to serve them or to preach to them. That is why the rabbis in those days were of the entire community rather than of an individual synagogue, and perhaps that is why rabbis preached only twice a year. The effort to make it easier to observe the laws by streamlining them brings to mind a statement by Kurt Lewin, who said, "In my opinion, Jews have made a great mistake in assuming that to keep a large membership one should demand as little as possible from the individual. Strong groups are not built that way" (*Resolving Social Conflicts*, p. 199). Furthermore, once the restrictions against traveling to the synagogue are lifted it will of course mean that the ban on the use of the automobile is lifted entirely, eventually turning Shabbat into a weekend.

Experience in the army can serve as a guide in that respect. The chaplains understood at the very outset that their work would entail *hilul Shabbat,* particularly riding. Now, after the war, it may be told that a great number of our chaplains—and I include the Orthodox—once they started using their cars used them for pleasure too, and for purposes they would not have dreamt of had they not started to use the car at all. Evidently they followed the principle, *keivan shehutra l'tzorekh hutra nami shelo l'tzorekh* ("once it is permitted when necessary, we also permit it when it is not necessary"). And you may be sure that every layman—with notable exceptions to be sure—will reason in the same manner.

On the subject of changes let me quote from a book published a few years ago in England, but known very little in America. It was written by a rabbi who, although he may not know it or admit it, surely seems to have an approach that we could accept:

> Being a Jew does not mean that one has to prove the compatibility of Judaism with a life built on a non-Jewish foundation. It is, therefore, not right to call for the reform of Judaism under pressure of the hard facts of modern life. It is certainly very uncomfortable to be a Jew in the midst of a Christian world, but a reform of Judaism on that ground alone means sacrificing Judaism on the altar of Christian civilization for the sake of individual comfort. The only justification for a call for reform would be the exigencies of a Jewish controlled environment; for instance, a modern Jewish life in an autonomous Eretz Yisrael. The necessities of Jewish life are the necessities of Judaism. The demands of a Jewish-owned environment are justified demands on Judaism and must be satisfied by Judaism. But exigencies arising out of the "Christian existence" of Jews in the midst of Western civilization, demands resulting from the difference between the rhythm of

Judaism and some other civilization, these are no problems of theology or philosophy; they are part of the great Jewish tragedy. They all go back to the political problem of the *Galut*. Naturally enough they are influencing the religious and cultural atmosphere of Judaism. As to them we say: rather should we perish in defending Judaism than subject it to a reform that can only mean dissolution and destruction. Our "Christian existence" is no reason whatever to reform Judaism. As long as Jews live in *Galut* the conflict between Judaism and non-Jewish sorroundings will remain; we shall have to endure the strain, that cannot be helped. . . .

Any further development of Judaism is only possible by the creation somewhere on this earth, of a complete Jewish environment, i.e., a reality that is wide enough to embrace the whole existence of the Jewish national unit. Only by the creation of such a Jewish environment can we give back to Torah the great partnership of Life which alone is able to free Judaism from its present Galut-conditioned rigidity, and create the circumstances in evolution will again be possible." (*Towards Historic Judaism*, E. Berkovitz p. 34 f.)

This book was published in England in 1943. It is quite evident that we cannot go along completely with the author. This spells a negation of the *galut* that we cannot accept for the simple reason that two thousand years of life in the diaspora has proven the contrary; has proven false the contention that only in Israel is a real Jewish life possible. And yet the statement points to a certain truth which must be taken into consideration. We speak today a great deal about organic thinking and the organic community. Let us also add the expression, organic growth of religion, to our vocabulary. Our growth in America is in many respects artificial, mechanical, organizational. In Israel it is or could be organic. In other words, in Israel it is part of life while in America it is not. Hence, we have not discovered the proper formula which would help us change the law and yet preserve it.

Let me illustrate this difference with a concrete example. During a recent visit to Israel I had an opportunity to discuss the question of changes in the regulations of religious practice in Israel. My conversation was with a distinguished member of ha-Poel ha-Mizrahi, who was also a member of the cabinet, and I asked him regarding the operation on Shabbat of public utilities and other public services that cannot be interrupted. He felt confident that some modus vivendi will be found which will not violate the sanctity of Shabbat and, at the same time, will permit the necessary operations to continue. He cited the following example. In Tel Aviv the office of postmaster became vacant. The position was offered to a member of the Mizrahi because, by party agreement, it was their turn. The gentleman refused the offer because it would entail a violation of the Sabbath. This was an untenable situation, and the religious group thereupon had a meeting and came to the following conclusion. There should be no position in the Israeli government which an observant Jew could not accept. If it entails work that can be avoided on Shabbes then it should be avoided even if the holder of the position is not an observant Jew. On the other hand, if the work is indispensable, then a religious Jew too should be able to perform it on Shabbes.

Here is a workable formula which makes good logic and which stems from the realities of life in Israel.

Another instance which interested me very much is the following. Speaking to a gentleman, a recent arrival from Slovakia, whence came the most pious and observant Jews of today, and a member of the Agudah to boot, he shocked me with the following remarks. He claimed that if he were a member of a religious lawmaking body he would search for ways and means of permitting riding on Shabbes, and for the following reasons. First, the people work hard all week and Shabbes is the only day of rest and recreation. A new generation has arisen, even among the pious, that does not consider spending Shabbes afternoons by reciting the Psalms or studying the portion of the week as recreation. Physical recreation and sports attract modern youth from all segments of the community and cannot be eliminated from their lives. Furthermore, social life is possible only on Shabbes. Of course the rabbinate has tried to persuade the authorities to add an additional afternoon during the week on which shops and factories would be closed in order to provide just for that. At present, this is difficult because of the urgency of the work to be done. Remarks like these came to me as a revelation of the currents now prevalent in Israel.

In both cases, it becomes apparent what can be done where traditional religion is still part of life and a way of life. Our problem in America is quite different. When the situation will be analogous in America we shall be able to employ similar methods.

Harold Laski, in the chapter on religion in America, in his well-known book on American democracy makes this remark: "I venture to think that the American Churches, as a mass expression of American Life, produce religiosity and not religion." Laski meant by this that the main work of the churches in America has been to add an ecclesiastical aura to the American creed of success. Religion, on the other hand, "is the inner and passionate impulse which drives those who possess it beyond and above themselves to an evaluation where they can conquer the immediate desire, and the temporary caprice, in their search for the fraternal relation with all who suffer and all who are broken by the tragedy of a pain they cannot face. Religion in this sense can never compromise with the world; it must be willing to break it or be broken by it rather than to yield the imperative passion in which it finds its supreme expression."

If we shall not be able to bring about a solid foundation of piety and observance at least in a portion of our people then we, too, shall at best create a religiosity, a certain sentimental aura around certain ceremonials, but not religion.

In his book, *Heshbon ha-Nefesh*, Mr. Zalmen Yefroikin, the author, asks: Whence do we Jews manage to get so many freethinkers? (*Avu nemt zich bei uns Yidden azoi fiel freidenker?*). This question was directed to the Yiddish intelligentsia. We would paraphrase this question with, "Where did we get so many people indifferent to religion?" It is a very disturbing question because the tribe is much larger among us than among our non-Jewish neighbors. The reasons for it are patent and we need not belabor them. The fact stands out and in any consideration about the future of Judaism it looms large and asks for a solution.

In the *Ethics of the Fathers* we have the statement: "Qualify thyself for the study of the Torah, since the knowledge of it is not an inheritance of thine, and let thy deeds be done for the sake of Heaven" (2:17). In the style of the *magid* of old we shall ask, "What continuity or connection is there between the two statements?" And we shall answer in the style of the *magid* as follows: "There are two Torahs. There is the Torah which is "thine inheritance" that is handed down from generation to generation. And there is the Torah which is not "thine inheritance," which is not handed down but is an innovation necessitated by the times and the new circumstances. Such a Torah needs special application. (The Hebrew term is *v'hatkein atzmakha* from the root *tikkun*.) And for such a Torah we have the special warning, "And let all thy deeds be done for the sake of Heaven." The innovation must be rooted in *yirat shamayim*, otherwise it is not warranted. This *yirat shamayim* can come from an adequate philosophy of religion and a rationale for its tenets, a rationale that is cogent to the modern mind and which make religion relevant. Then we can implant a regimen of *mitzvot*."

The Talmud asks why, in the recitation of the *Shema*, we say first the *v'ahavta*, and then *v'haya im shamoa*, and answers, that *kabalat ol malkhut shamayim* ("the acceptance of the yoke of the Kingdom of Heaven") must precede the *kabalat ol mitzvot* ("the acceptance of the *mitzvot*"). This should be our guide. We must convince ourselves first of the worthwhileness of *kabalat ol malkhut shamayim*, and then the *kabalat ol mitzvot* will have a better chance of realization.

INDEX

187